The LIVERPOOL Stage

First Published 1996

The Liverpool Stage
Copyright Harold Ackroyd 1996

Typeset, produced, designed and
published by:
Amber Valley Print Centre,
Erdington, West Midlands

ISBN 0 9514235 3 3

Harold
Ackroyd

The
LIVERPOOL
Stage

ACKNOWLEDGEMENTS

Research into the early history of theatres in Liverpool began with *Annals of the Liverpool Stage* (1908) by R.J. Broadbent, after which the principal sources of information were the local newspapers, *The Liverpool Echo, Daily Post, Bootle Times, Crosby Herald* and in earlier years, the *Liverpool Mercury*, the *Liverpool Review* and the *Liverpool Courier*. In this connection I wish to acknowledge with thanks, the assistance of the staff at the Liverpool Reference Library and the micro-film unit at the Liverpool Central Library, also the Crosby Reference Library.

I also wish to thank the undermentioned who contributed information and photographs:

Yvonne Bennett de Rothschild, formerly with Livepool Playhouse Repertory Company
Crosby Reference Library (drawings on page 112 and 113)
J Gonzales, Liverpool (photographs on pages 53 and 62)
R Hamblet, Meols, Wirral (photograph on page 88)
C Hunt, *Liverpool Echo*
Liverpool Central Reference Library (photographs on pages12, 16, 17, 19, 21, 23, 26, 32, 45, 52, 55, 57, 74, 76, 84, 85, 86, 100, 106, 107 and 108)
Barbara and June Martin, Birkdale (photographs on pages 72 and 75)
Neptune Theatre (photograph on page 96)
F K Oliver, theatre historian, Birkenhead
M Taylor, cinema and theatre historian, Liverpool (photographs on pages 66, 79 and 115)
Arthur Woods (programmes on pages 46 and 48)
P Woolley, local historian, (photograph on page 82)
M Yelland, theatre historian, Southport (photographs on pages 15, 24, 31, 44, 61, 63, 64, 65, 69, 77, 89, 94, 102, 103 and 105)

All unacknowledged photographs are from the author's own collection.

CONTENTS

THE ROYAL HIPPODROME

THEATRES IN CHRONOLOGICAL ORDER OF OPENING

Date of opening	Date of closure	Theatre name	
1750	c1788	Drury Lane Theatre	11
1772	1802	Theatre Royal, Williamson Sq.	12
1795	1805	Christian Street Circus	14
		The Olympic Circus	
		Queen's Theatre	
1862	c1900	Adelphi Theatre	
1803	1885	The New Theatre Royal	15
c1825		The Pantheon Theatre	19
1829	1850	The Liver Theatre	
c1825	1843	The Sans Pareil Theatre	20
1826		Cooke's New Circus	21
1840		The Royal Amphitheatre	
1881	1933	Royal Court Theatre	
1832	1865	Zoological Gardens Theatre	27
1842	-	Prince of Wales Theatre	27
1846	1860	The Hop	27
1840s	-	The Penny Hop	27
1847		Parthenon Music Hall	27
1907	1908	Theatre Moderne	
1850		Royal Collosseum Theatre	29
		Saunder's Theatre of Varieties	
		City Theatre of Varieties	
		New Grand Theatre and Opera House	
		Queen's Theatre	
	1916	Kelly's Theatre	
c1850	c1890	The Queen's Hall/Bijou Theatre and Opera House	32
1852	c1900	The Royal Park Theatre	32
1859		Theatre Variete	32
1868		St. James's Hall	
1896	1898	The Tivoli Palace of Varieties	
1906		The New Tivoli Palace of Varieties	
1909	1959	Palais de Luxe cinema	
1861	1905	Prince of Wales Theatre	36
1860s	Music Halls	Bell's English and American Hippodrome Circus	40
		Princess Theatre/Victoria Music Hall	40
		Casino Temperance Hall	
		The Liver Music Hall	41
		Royal Alhambra Music Hall	41
		Eagle Music Hall	41
	1879	The New Royal Theatre/Alhambra Music Hall	41
	c1879	The Cambridge Music Hall	41
		The Oxford Music Hall	41
		The Constellation Music Hall	41
1866		New Prince of Wales Theatre	42
1867		Royal Alexandra Theatre	
1896	1924	Empire Theatre	

Date of opening	Date of closure	Theatre name	Page no.
1866		The Star Music Hall	45
1896		The Star Theatre of Varieties	
1898		The Star Theatre	
1911		Liverpool Repertory Theatre	
1917		Playhouse Theatre	
1867		The Prince Patrick Hall	54
1868		The Wellington Hall	
1874	c1900	The Gaiety Theatre	
1869	1877	Rotunda Music Hall	54
1878	1940	Rotunda Theatre	
1875	early 1900s	Sefton Theatre	58
1912	1924	Park Royal Picture House	
1882	-	Haymarket Music Hall	58
1887		Westminster Music Hall	59
1908		Westminster Hall Cinema	
1932	1941	Doric Cinema	
1888	1976	Shakespeare Theatre	59
1888		Theatre Royal, Anfield	68
1920	1965	Royal Super Cinema	
1890		Paddington Palace of Varieties	69
1911		Coliseum de Luxe (Cinema)	
1926	1956	New Coliseum Cinema	
1890		Royal Muncaster Theatre	70
1912		New Princes Theatre	
1921	c1948	Strand Cinema	
1892		Roscommon Music Hall	73
1911	1958	Roscommon Cinema	
1892		Royal Palace of Varieties	73
1893		Park Palace of Varieties	74
1911		Park Palace Kinematodrome	
	1959	Park Palace Cinema	
1897	1932	Lyric Theatre	77
1902	1931	Royal Hippodrome Theatre	78
1931	1970	Hippodrome Cinema	
1905	1925	Olympia Theatre	81
1925	1939	Olympia Super Cinema	
1906	1977	The David Lewis Theatre	84
1908	1961	Pavilion Theatre	87
1909		Winter Gardens Theatre, Bootle	90
1911	1923	Apollo Theatre/Cinema	
1909		Bijou Theatre	92
1912	1922	Bijou Electric Palace/Cinema	
1911	1941	Metropole Theatre	92
1913		Crane Hall	96
1938	1968	Crane Theatre	
1968		Neptune Theatre	
1915	1918	Empire Theatre, Garston	97
1918	1962	Empire Cinema, Garston	
1922	1931	Winter Gardens Theatre, Waterloo	98
1931	1965	Winter Gardens Cinema	
1925		Empire Theatre, Liverpool	100

Date of opening	Date of closure	Theatre name	Page no.
1938		Royal Court Theatre	104
1964	1977	Everyman Theatre	110
1975		The Civic Hall, Crosby	112
1977		The New Everyman Theatre	114
1980		Unity Theatre	116

INTRODUCTION

Records indicate that long before the opening of Liverpool's first theatres in the mid 16th century, entertainment including drama was presented only at private venues, before the Norman Conquest in 1066 at West Derby Castle, and seven years later at Liverpool castle, constructed in the area which today includes the Queen Victoria monument and Castle Street. These performances, which included drama, were given by the Norman jongleurs, who were itinerant singers and reciters, but whilst their repertoire was described as highly sophisticated, that of their successors, played at the time of markets and fairs, became crude and very different from their predecessors. From these performers was derived the name of Juggler Street, later renamed High Street, in the original built up area of Liverpool founded as a borough by King John in 1207. This consisted of Water Street, Dale Street, Castle Street, High Street, Chapel Street and Tithebarn Street.

From the 16th century, the Stanleys, Earls of Derby, were almost continually devoted patrons of the drama, which they often enjoyed, mainly at their seats of Knowsley, of Lathom near Ormskirk, also at their stronghold of the Tower of Liverpool while they awaited favourable winds for sailing to their kingdom of the Isle of Man. It is believed that some of the more privileged burgesses (citizens with full municipal rights) were occasionally permitted to attend the dramatic performances at Knowsley and in the Tower Of Liverpool, but those of a lower station in life had no such opportunities. Even the burgesses had in general to provide their dramatic entertainments from other sources, and in this they received little encouragement from the authorities. An excellent reason for this is provided by the fact that by Act of Parliament, stage players who were not licensed in the companies of the nobles were declared to be vagabonds and rogues. They could be sent to the House of Correction, whipped or be burned with a hot iron, the breadth of an English shilling with a great Roman "R" on the left shoulder, which remained as the permanent mark of a rogue. They might alternatively be banished, executed as felons, or imprisoned in the stocks near the High Cross outside the Town Hall, opposite Juggler Street. But these severe measures were effective for a limited time only due to the great love of drama in Tudor Liverpool, for in 1571 the burgesses decided to licence wandering players providing that they did not bring into the town anything to the distress of the Queen's subjects without license, for the time being of Mr. Mayor.

By this time the borough was already a patron of the drama with two civic theatres, one indoors on the second floor of the Town Hall, also used as a court, and the other, originally in the municipal cockfight pit, constructed by the borough in 1567 as an attraction to the town for entertainment of gentlemen and others. The plays performed in the Town Hall, also known as the Common Hall, were produced with the encouragement of the Mayor, by the schoolmaster with his scholars, who were paid according to their expenses. In 1571 it was discovered that the upper floor was not sufficiently strong for the presentation of plays which included dancing, and these were reluctantly forbidden by the Mayor for the safety of the building. The Cockpit Yard, between the end of Drury Lane and Moor Street, became at an apparently unrecorded date, Liverpool's first humble building to be used for dramatic entertainment. The auditorium with dimensions of 50ft by 20ft was constructed with a small gallery. Seating on the ground floor was by benches on either side of the stage. The walls were whitewashed and the only lighting was by candles. The theatre was situated midway between the rival strongholds, the Castle and the Tower, where the troops were billeted, and the area was therefore a centre of disorder. The association of this with the theatre resulted in it's closure during the civil war of the 1640s, but reopening took place after the restoration to the throne of King Charles II in 1660. The original theatre area around present day Water Street, later including the Old Ropery and Drury Lane theatres, remained for 200 years the centre of dramatic entertainment.

The Cockpit Yard Theatre survived to the early 19th century, later, c1810 the building again became a venue for cock fights, then demolished for the erection of a corn warehouse on the site.

Another early playhouse which originated as a cockpit was the Blackberry Lane theatre, on the left hand side of the lane, now Eberle Street from Dale Street. Whilst there is no information regarding the opening of the theatre, it can be stated to have been open in the early 1740s, when a company of players performed in *The Tempest* for an unbroken run of 30 nights, to the great satisfaction of the audience. Another reference indicates that in 1742 the Irish Players from Dublin, appeared there, breaking their journey in Liverpool on their way to the Preston Guild. The only further information is that the building was converted into a warehouse at an unknown date.

The growth of trade with America and Africa led to the expansion of the town with the emergence of a new class of merchants and entrepreneurs, which provided a new powerful patron and influence in the development of drama in Liverpool. A symbol of this new class was Alderman Thomas Steers, Mayor in 1739, and engineer of the first dock, named the Old Dock, which laid the foundation for the rapid increase in trade. Thomas Steers was also responsible for the construction in 1740 of the first real theatre in Liverpool, as understood by the term, the Old Ropery, in the gap caused by the demolition of the Castle of Liverpool, on the site where the New Market was also constructed. On land cutting through the present Brunswick Street the building consisted of two storeys, the theatre on the ground floor, which could be rented for £25 per annum, whilst the upper storey was occupied for a time by a dancing academy. Still in an age before newspapers and play-bills, the only recorded information is that performances were given by an excellent company of players of the Smock Alley Company from Dublin in August 1742. This was occasioned by the fact that due to contrary winds, their journey by sailing ship had been delayed, and arriving at Liverpool too late for the Preston Guild, and with their finances exhausted, they obtained permission from the Mayor of Liverpool to perform in the Old Ropery, and to solicit the gentry of the town to patronise the performances. So great was their success that they made at least one further appearance the following year, and connections with the Dublin stage are known to have continued in the 1750s by players of the Crow Street Theatre. They crossed over to England, visiting Liverpool, Manchester and Chester etc. at the time of the Dublin recess between the end of June and the beginning of October. The Old Ropery building was later used as a warehouse, and demolished in 1786 prior to the construction of Brunswick Street.

During the war of the Austrian Succession, 1739-1748, Liverpool's privateers were enormously successful, and the riches they brought to the town laid the foundation for great steps forward in the development of drama. This benefited considerably by the opening c1749 of the new, and largest theatre to date, the Drury Lane, the last to be erected in that which for 200 years was known as the theatre area. It is now remembered only by the still remaining thoroughfare of that name between Water Street and James Street, but the new Liverpool which was being built in the mid 18th century is still represented by the Town Hall, extended to form the present building in 1795, after serious fire damage to the

original, designed by John Wood of Bath and opened in 1754.

Although the first half of the 19th century saw the replacement of the stagecoach in 1831 by the important railway link between Liverpool and Manchester, and the beginning of an age of reform, leading to the Reform Act of 1832, and the Municipal Act of 1835, it was nevertheless also the beginning of a squalid period in the history of Liverpool with the creation of slums. It is recorded that between 1771 and 1841 the population had increased from 34,000 to 250,000, which resulted in an enormous demand for entertainment as an escape from the misery of everyday life. It was fortunate therefore that an increase in the number of theatres was made possible due to the passing by the government of a new act in 1843 for the licensing of all theatres, thereby ending the 70 years' theatrical monopoly of the Theatre Royal.

The Liver Theatre in Church Street then became the first in England to be licensed under the new Act, re-opening as the Royal Liver, after which the number of theatres considerably increased. But although the Theatre Royal's monopoly was broken with several theatres in competition, it transpired that, as had been claimed by

its management, there was not sufficient support for drama to keep them viable, and the Liver in 1850 was among the closures of the smaller theatres during subsequent years.

Liverpool has an impressive record of Shakespearian productions, *Macbeth* was acted in 1714, later, *The Tempest*, also numerous productions of *Hamlet,* and among these, according to local dramatic criticism, written by Sir Edward Russell, editor of the *Liverpool Daily Post*. That of 1885 with Sir Henry Irving was the classic, but due to the fact that Irving subjugated all his company to himself, the truest Shakespearian acting was that of Hunt's Old Vic at the Royal Court Theatre in 1950, which included Michael Redgrave, Miles Malleson and Mark Dignam.

During the latter half of the 19th century, as an alternative to the stage plays of the legitimate theatre, the music hall grew in popularity. Notable among these, opened in 1866, was the Star in Williamson Square. Four years later another popular form of entertainment, the minstrel show, reached its peak with Sam Hague's troup during the 25 years at the St. James's Hall in Lime Street. Towards the end of the nineteenth century came twice nightly variety entertainment, for which the leading theatre was the Empire. Then in the early years of the present century, the opening of the Royal Hippodrome Theatre of Varieties (1902) was closely followed by that of the Olympia (1905), Liverpool's all time largest theatres, both designed for all types of 'live' entertainment.

First shown in 1896 as a supporting item at many theatres and music halls, motion pictures represented strong competition, especially from 1912, when the first two purpose built cinemas, the Picture House, Lime Street and the Liverpool Picture House, Clayton Square were opened. In addition to these, the Tivoli Palace of Varieties had become the Palais de Luxe cinema, which remained open for over 50 years, the only such conversion in the city centre. Those of the suburbs survived as cinemas for varying lengths of time, and closed for various reasons as indicated in their individual histories.

GAZETEER OF THEATRES

1750
THE DRURY LANE THEATRE

Named after the famous London theatre, this theatre was erected c1750 on the east side of the new thoroughfare name Drury Lane between the Old Ropery Theatre and the present Brunswick Street, and for a similar reason, the style and title of Covent Garden was given to an adjacent thoroughfare, which also still exists between Water Street and Chapel Street.

The theatre was a structure of plain brick about 81ft long and 48ft in width. The auditorium consisted of a pit, over which the gallery extended for some distance and was considered to be the best part of the house for viewing a performance. Nevertheless admission to the pit was 2/-, and to the gallery 1/-. There were no boxes but as at the Cockpit Yard Theatre there were seats on either side of the stage for the better class patrons. Candles still provided the only illumination for the stage and the auditorium, above which they were fitted in circular wooden frames suspended from the ceiling, those above the audience being snuffed out during the acts. The use of candles for lighting was continued until the opening of the Theatre Royal, Williamson Square in 1772. The Drury Lane had no dressing room accommodation, the artists having to change dress on a bench behind the scenery.

A surprising metropolitan custom at that time was to have two soldiers from a regiment stationed in the town, hired at one shilling each per night to stand on either side of the stage, hands resting on their firelocks to keep order until the final fall of the curtain at the end of the performance.

At a time several years before Liverpool's first newspapers and known playbills, hence the exact opening date cannot be stated, the town's principal theatre, the Drury Lane opened c1750 under the joint management of Mr. William Gibson and a Mr. Ridout, both members of the London Covent Garden Theatre company. Whilst their management was greatly commended, and their acting highly esteemed by Liverpool playgoers, an aspect which did not meet with their approval was the practice of opening the doors at 5pm when a large audience was expected, and therefore to ensure a good position, patrons had to wait up to two hours for the play to begin!

At that time Liverpool was a popular seaside resort and for many years numerous wealthier families came for the bathing season during the summer months. This addition to the population provided a boost to theatre attendances, a fact generally known to the players, who made the journey to Liverpool to earn money when the Theatre Royals in London were closed. From the time of opening 1750 until 1756 there is no record of those who appeared at Drury Lane, for which the first advertisement appeared in the first edition of *Williamson's Advertiser* on 28 May 1756, the earliest known press advertisement for a theatre, which announced - *"By Comedians from the Theatre Royal in London at this Theatre in Liverpool. During the months of June, July and August next will be performed a variety of the best plays on Mondays, Wednesdays and Fridays."* The oldest known playbill announced *"At the Theatre in Drury Lane, this present Friday, 4th of June 1756 - A comedy called The Constant Couple or A Trip to the Jubilee to which will be added a farce called The Virgin Unmasked or An Old Man taught Wisdom. The Gallery doors to be opened at five, and the pit at six. To begin exactly at seven. Prices, pit two shillings, gallery one shilling."* To which was added - *"Not any money under the full price to be taken during the whole performance, nor any servants to be admitted into the gallery without paying."* Formerly it had been the custom at London and provincial theatres for servants of those seated in the boxes to be admitted to the gallery free of charge, but this ceased due to the noisy behaviour of the servants, and gave the management a good excuse to close the gallery to servants and to charge admission to all who entered.

The theatre was closed for reconstruction from 5th September 1758 to June 1759, during which time boxes placed around the pit were added to the auditorium. These provided a partition between the better class patrons and druken sailors, and by paying two shillings they had the honour of associating with their employers and families. An alteration to the gallery is indicated by the fact that, according to a statement at that time, prior to the alterations it extented very far over the pit.

Although it cannot be confirmed, according to an official source the date of re-opening was 22nd June 1759 with a change of name to the New Theatre in Drury Lane, at which were presented the comedy, *The Conscious Lovers* and the farce, *The Lying Valet.*

The theatre was still under the control of Messrs Gibson and Ridout, and remained so until early in 1761 when the latter retired due to ill health and died in the same year. William Gibson then became sole manager of the house, which during the ensuing ten years reverted to its former name, the Drury Lane Theatre.

At the end of the 1760s, Mr. Gibson concentrated his energies on plans for a new theatre which would be worthy of the town, presenting a petition to the Corporation of Liverpool urging them to support his application to Parliament for a Theatre Royal to be erected in Liverpool, to which the Royal Letters Patent would be granted. This gave to the theatre exclusive right in the choice of plays or other entertainments over any other theatre in the town.

There was considerable delay on the part of the Corporation in supporting Mr. Gibson's application, although they had refused to renew the licence of the Drury Lane for the reason that its situation was then a very dangerous place, approached by narrow streets frequented by thieves. After the petition had received on 9th November 1769 the Common Seal, which was necessary to enable H.M. King George III to grant his Letters Patent, there was a further delay of over twelve months before the petition was passed by both the House of Lords and the House of Commons. Later, on 30th April 1771, William Gibson was granted permission to establish for a term of twenty one years, a Theatre Royal in Liverpool, and to keep a company of Comedians for His Majesty's Service in Liverpool. A designation only applied to those players who performed at the patent theatres, at that time a distinct and much sought honour.

In 1771 the house in Drury Lane was styled as the Theatre Royal with a company known as His Majesty's Comedians, most of whom were from the Theatre Royal, Drury Lane, London, but among the others, noticeably absent was William Gibson, then lying seriously ill at his residence in Everton. His death on 21st August 1771 was considered a great loss to the world of the theatre in Liverpool and it was tragic that after his great efforts during the previous years he did not live to see the opening of his new Theatre Royal in Williamson Square.

The patent for the performance of plays in addition to his other assets was left by William Gibson in his will to Mrs. Elizabeth Bennett, formerly of the Drury Lane Theatre, whom he appointed sole executrix.

The theatre in Drury Lane remained open for many years after the opening of the new Theatre Royal, but the performances were only occasional with stage plays performed principally by amateurs. Whilst it is not possible to trace the actual date of closure, available information indicates that the building together with other property was purchased in 1788 from a Mrs. Chapman, and partly demolished, the remaining portion being converted into a warehouse. Later leased by the Corporation as an engine house at a yearly rental of £3, by 1829 this part had also been demolished.

1772
THE THEATRE ROYAL,
Williamson Square

The cost of erecting this theatre, estimated at about £6,000 was raised in shares of £200 each, bearing 5 per cent interest, and entitling the holder to a silver, free admission ticket. All the necessary money for the venture was subscribed in

less than one hour after the list had been opened, and on 3rd June 1771 the foundation stone was laid by the Mayor of Liverpool, Mr. John Sparling. This event was little over two months before the death of the founder, William Gibson, and almost exactly one year prior to the opening of Liverpool's first theatre to be opened with Royal Letters Patent, granted by His Majesty King George III.

The new theatre, to the plans of architect Sir William Chambers, was described as a large and handsome building, elegantly finished both externally and internally, and with excellent acoustic properties. In line with the houses on either side the 60ft frontage of red brick was surmounted by a full width gable, with an artistic pediment in which was featured a large carving in stone of the Royal Coat of Arms. Below this the brickwork was relieved by the stonework surrounds of the doors and windows, which, in the centre at first floor level, a group of windows was divided by stonework into three sections, forming a tall, arched window in the centre. In view of the considerable width of the frontage the central main entrance at the head of a flight of stone steps, although narrow, containing only two glass panelled doors beneath a small archway, was nevertheless an impressive architec-

tural feature, flanked by columns and surmounted by a pediment. At the extreme left and right, also at the head of stone steps, entrance/exit ways were provided.

From the main entrance access to the boxes was from the centre, whilst on one side a passage led to the pit, and on the other to the gallery in the square-shaped auditorium, lit only by candles and oil lamps, as were all parts of the building, gas not being introduced until early in the nineteenth century.

Although the patent for the performance of plays in Liverpool had been bequeathed by William Gibson to his dear and best beloved friend, Elizabeth Bennett, apparently she did not wish to take an active part in the running of the Theatre Royal since she leased it for a period of 14 years to Messrs. Joseph Younger and George Mattocks at a yearly rental of £140. Both lessees were capable actors and favourites with Liverpool playgoers. The former had been a prompter at London's Covent Garden Theatre, and the latter had made his first Liverpool appearances at the Drury Lane Theatre in 1767.

The opening of the Theatre Royal on the Friday evening of 5th June 1772 was an auspicious occasion, attended by all the elite of the town. Following the reading of the opening prologue written by George Colman, the elder, and spoken by lessee Joseph Younger, the performance commenced with the tragedy of *Mahomet* which was followed by the farce, *The Deuce is in Him*. The price of admission to the boxes was 3/6d, the pit 2/6d and the gallery 1/-.

The original arrangements for the booking of performers restricted the opening of the theatre to the summer months, commencing when the two London patent theatres, the Drury Lane and Covent Garden were closed, and concluded when those theatre were about to open for the winter season. Although the London performers were committed under heavy penalties to remain at the Theatre Royal for the entire dramatic season, the arrangement soon became troublesome and expensive due to the lengthy journeys back to London by stagecoach. It was therefore necessary for the players to leave Liverpool hurriedly or take the risk of being late to open the season, and the problem was resolved by the engagement of more local artists.

It is recorded that at this time Liverpool presented a vastly different aspect from that of any time within living memory. There were pleasant landscapes, fruitful gardens and picturesque windmills dotted here and there on the hillside within a mile of the Town Hall, but the town was badly paved, drained and lit.

Within about a month of the opening, two accidents at the theatre were reported, but in the absence of newspapers at that time the only indication of when they occurred is from an authoritative source which states that they were during June/July 1772. A house on fire in Williamson Square caused a false alarm of fire to be raised in the theatre, and despite the efforts of the actors to reassure the audience that there was no danger, and the orchestra playing to allay their fears, one man rushed down the gallery stairs, fell and was killed, and several patrons accompanying him were injured. The second accident was comparatively minor, and occurred on the stage during the performance of a play entitled M*idas* during which the performers in their roles as gods and goddesses ascending to the celestial regions, fell down on to the stage, a carpen-

ter having failed to secure the bolt to the raised platform which parted in the middle.

By September 1772 the proprietors of the theatre consisted of a considerable number of professional gentlemen, merchants and other trades people, by whom, on the 14th a lease of the theatre for twenty years at a yearly rental of £281 was granted to Mrs. E. Bennett, to whom the founder William Gibson had, in his will, left the patent for the performance of plays. Towards the end of the 1770s however, the original lessees, Messrs. Younger and Mattocks, were again in control of the theatre and experiencing anxiety as a result of disturbances among the audience. This resulted in their taking legal action against several patrons, described as respectable townsmen, alleging they frequented the theatre with the intention of creating a disturbance, but the action was discontinued on payment of costs.

After the death of Joseph Younger on 4th September 1784 George Mattocks remained as sole lessee until 1786 when, financially ruined he was forced to retire from the management. In December 1786 a new patent for the performances was granted to George Case, one of the trustees of the proprietors, with a licence for fifteen years. There was a further change of lessee on 31st December 1792 when a seven year lease was granted to Mr. Francis Aickin, formerly associated with the Smock Alley Theatre, Dublin, and manager of the Theatre Royal from 1786. The lease at a yearly rental of £350 was thought to have been taken up by Mr. Aickin as a means of recouping the money he had expended for the work of raising the theatre roof for the construction of a new gallery and the construction of a colonnade over the principle entrance in Williamson Square.

Unfortunately for Francis Aickin the Theatre Royal was soon struggling to survive in difficult times, for in 1793, when Shakespeare's *As You Like It* was being performed came the French declaration of war. Whilst this generated patriotic enthusiasm, it also brought about the problem of unruliness in the theatre due to the change of policy to a far less refined type of entertainment with plays in 1794 such as *The*

Liverpool Prize or *An Offering To Britannia*. So attrocious did the behaviour of audiences become that on 24th September 1795, the editor of *Gore's Advertiser* expressed astonishment that no steps had been taken to curb the disorderly proceedings which took place nightly in the gallery, from which patrons in the pit were pelted with various objects throughout the performance. Their safety was even put in danger by drunkards traversing around the outside of the gallery rails, and on the date in question, one man repeatedly attempted to throw one of the chandeliers into the pit! All of which resulted in the evacuation of several boxes!

Towards the end of the 18th century, the pit also became the scene of riot, confusion and excessive drinking, but in spite of the disorder the Theatre Royal continued to be popular with rich and poor alike, for as revealed in an anecdote related by the popular Liverpool actress, Harriet Mellon - *Side by side with brutality was sentimentality.*

The conditions under which the Theatre Royal survived worsened in 1797 due to a threat of invasion when a French frigate landed 1,200 troops on the Welsh coast, causing a rush to get out of Liverpool by the stage coaches or other means of transport. The theatre nevertheless remained open, and in 1798 made fun of Napoleon's desire to invade England in a one-act musical play *The Raft* or *Both Sides of the Water*. In 1799 such plays as the one act musical *The Maid of Liverpool* or *The Royal Tar* continued to attract rough audiences, the gallery being mainly attended by drunken sailors and their sweethearts, who came for no other purpose than to drink gin and crack nuts!

Whether or not entirely attributable to Francis Aickin, his term as lessee saw the decline of the Theatre Royal, not only due to the bad behaviour of the audience, but also the deteriorating condition of the theatre which, it was alleged, had been the result of the excessive economy in its operation. One of the most important incentives to improvement of the Theatre Royal was the competition provided by the Christian Street Circus opened in 1795, for which the public were gratified by the best set of entertainments remembered in Liverpool. At a time of still decreasing attendances in 1802 the proprietors submitted plans to the corporation for alteration and enlargement of the theatre. They also took the opportunity provided by the expiration on 1st January 1803 of Francis Aickin's lease to invite proposals from any persons who would be interested in taking it up. From many applications William Thomas Lewis and Thomas Knight were selected by the proprietors and granted a lease for 14 years at an annual rental of £1,500. It is noteworthy that although Francis Aickin offered £100 more than the new Lessees he was turned down for the reason that he was so disliked in Liverpool as a result of the decline of the theatre during his former lesseeship.

Responding to criticism of its condition and the challenge of its rival, the Theatre Royal was closed on 24th November 1802. The last of 36 benefit performances in that year brought the total receipts to £5,053, of which those of the final evening amounted to £241 with the plays *Boaden's Voice of Nature*, *The Midnight Hour* and the comic opera *Tom Thumb*.

Although it had been formerly indicated that the theatre was to be altered and enlarged, it was in fact demolished and the building of the new theatre was commenced in December 1802.

> **1795**
> **THE CHRISTIAN STREET CIRCUS/OLYMPIC CIRCUS/ QUEEN'S THEATRE/ADELPHI THEATRE/ADELPHI CINEMA**

This was owned by a Mr. T. Tinkler, who had taken over a livery stables being built in Christian Street and in 1789 added an undercover ring, which was run as a riding school and arena for equestrian shows before opening in 1795 as the popular Christian Street Circus.

In January 1803 the Circus opened under the management of a Mr. Davis with performances including horsemanship, tight-rope dancing, equestrian exercises, and Mr. Davis also gave riding lessons but was forced to close in March 1803.

Mr. Davis took on three partners, Messrs. Parker, Smith and Crossman and re-opened the Circus on 23rd April 1804, the partners were themselves actors and an actress, and in effect the Circus was being run on a short term basis by this small theatre group and led to its closure for long periods.

With the same management it re-opened on 1st April 1805 as the Olympic Circus which proved successful and towards the end of 1806 it came under the direction of Mr. John Banks of the Theatre Royal. At the close of the season in April 1808, the Circus was enlarged, much altered and improved by Mr. John Foster, architect of St. Luke's Church and Liverpool Custom House as well as numerous other buildings in Liverpool. Appearing as almost a new building the facade was ornamented with genuine pilasters, capitals and bases, whereas previously these had only been painted but the entire scheme of improvements originated as a result of the roof being considered unsafe, which determined the proprietors to commit themselves to a great amount of reconstruction. The walls were increased in height to allow for a second tier of boxes, from which an excellent view of the stage and the riding area could be obtained. Styled as the upper boxes, they were reached by a flight of wide stairs from a commodious lounge. The new roof was constructed on the latest and most scientific principles of carpentry by a method which gave every truss a double bearing on the wall. The wooden columns which had supported the boxes were removed and replaced by others of neat cast iron to give stronger support, and the circus auditorium then formed three complete tiers or storeys for the audience. The lower of these, level with the ground floor, was styled as the gallery whilst on the second floor were the boxes, and on the third, the upper boxes. The entire auditorium was redecorated and from the front of the proscenium a prominent cove joined the new ceiling which was elegantly painted in fresco. Also, there were new doorways decorated with architraves and entablatures.

The entire scheme of alterations was to the design of the architect, Mr. John Foster and executed by Mr. Joseph Spencer, the contractor, who received the highest praise for his taste as an artist. It was stated that for elegance and accommodation the building was not surpassed or even equalled by any in the kingdom.

The Olympic Circus was run until 1812 by John Banks, then re-opened on 28th November 1813 by Messrs. Astley, Davis and Parker as the New Olympic Circus. The entertainment scene in Liverpool at that time was briefly summerised in the book entitled *Fifty Years of Green Room Gossip* by Walter Donaldson, who was also an actor, and made the comment that Liverpool in the summer had the Theatre Royal as the temple for tragedy, and in the winter, the Olympic Theatre for equestrian exercises, melodramas, ballets and pantomimes.

Remaining under the ownership of Messrs. Banks and Lewis, John Cooke and his equestrian company were engaged in December 1821 for the season until March 1822, then known as Cooke's Olympic Circus. Mr. Cooke later became the lessee and despite certain obstacles met with unprecedented success in his venture until 1825 when, due to the bursting of a sewer, the arena was immersed in water. Due to an irreconcilable dispute with the proprietors regarding liability for the cost of renovations, Mr. Cooke departed, and a committee of management was appointed, under whose direction the building was improved, strengthened newly decorated and renamed the Royal Olympic Circus which opened on 26th December 1825.

But the fortunes of the Olympic declined after the opening, in February 1826 by John Cooke, of his new circus in Great Charlotte Street and in 1831 the ring area of the Olympic was converted into a theatre with a pit in which seats with backs, as in other Liverpool theatres, were fitted. Appropriate to its new lease of life as a theatre an orchestra pit was constructed and the auditorium was redecorated.

The reopening of 26th December 1831 was as the Queen's Theatre by the comedian Harry Beverly with the play Harlequin Gulliver in which Beverley himself played the clown.

Although in close competition with Richard Malone Raymond and W.J. Hammond who managed the Liver Theatre in Church Street, the Queen's remained open for 15 years under the direction of several lessees and managers until 1846, when Mr. Hammond took over the Queen's. By that time it had become dirty and dingy. Deciding to revive the past glories of the theatre Mr. Hammond instituted the gutting of the interior followed by refitting and beautiful redecoration. The exterior which had been very plain with an ordinary brick front was given an ornamental face surmounted by several statues, although after one of these was blown down in the 1860s the others were removed.

considerably raised the character of the theatre, which then became known as the Adelphi, and was recognised as the home of spectacular drama. There was a change to pantomimes for the Christmas season and as in Mr. Hammond's time there were frequently lines of carriages approaching the theatre from as far as Islington.

Mr. Branson retired from management of the Adelphi in 1869, and was succeeded by Thomas Theodore Heath, formerly at the Colosseum, Paradise Street, who introduced variety entertainments, resulting in a change of name the following year to the Adelphi Music Hall & Theatre of

The final entertainment at the Adelphi was twice nightly variety, after which its closure in the early 1900s was attributed to the refusal of the city magistrates to grant a licence for a return to dramatic plays.

By about 1906 the building had been converted for use by the Liverpool Gymnastic Club Ltd., then six years later after another conversion it became the 650 seat Adelphi Cinema for which cinematograph licence was granted to a Mrs. Tarshish on 13th February 1912. The building was demolished in 1921 and the New Adelphi Cinema was erected on the site and opened in 1922 by the same proprietor. It remained open with several changes of ownership until 1941, when the building was destroyed during one of the many air raids on Merseyside during World War II.

1803
THE NEW THEATRE ROYAL,
Williamson Square

Following the demolition of the old Theatre Royal, the new building was completed in only six months, and having been commenced in mid-winter, it was considered that great credit was reflected upon the active spirit, skill and perseverance of the architect, John Foster. In contrast to that of the old, the frontage of the new theatre was of stone and semi-circular, including the two separate principal entrances, and at the left hand-side a right angled section with the pit entrance. At first floor level, three principal windows, surmounted by panels bearing the Royal Coat of Arms and emblematical figures in bas relief were set within pairs of pilasters which extended up to the frieze.

The shape of the auditorium was nearly that of a horseshoe in which a good view of the performance could be obtained from all parts and the acoustics were considered to be excellent. Three tiers of balconies and boxes were supported by light cast iron pillars, the box fronts were painted with a type of silver lattice work and fitted with beautifully executed medallions. The fronts

With another change of name to the Theatre Royal Adelphi, the building was reopened by W.J. Hammond on Easter Monday, 13th April 1846, when there was a crowded house for the performance of *Romeo and Juliet,* although the prices had been increased, the best seats being 7/6d.

In July 1862 the theatre came under the control of William Scholes Branson, a former actor with the stock company of T.B. Sullivan at the Theatre Royal, Williamson Square, 15 years previously. Mr. Branson

Varieties under the control of Isaac de Frece as lessee and Harry de Frece as manager. In the mid 1870s there was a return to plays by a stock company when Edward Trevanion became proprietor and manager, inaugurating drama with two performances nightly. Mr. Trevanion remained in control of the theatre until his death in May 1887 after which it was continued by his executors with the assistance of Barry Stuart as business manager, who later became lessee and manager.

THEATRE ROYAL, LIVERPOOL.

On WEDNESDAY EVENING, JULY 28,

Will be performed Ben Jonson's Comedy, in Five Acts, of

EVERY MAN IN HIS HUMOUR.

Kiteley ....Mr. JOHN FORSTER	Cash ....Mr. AUGUSTUS DICKENS
Old Knowell....................................Mr. G. H. LEWES	Formal.. .... Mr. GEORGE CRUIKSHANK
Young Knowell (his Son)......Mr. FREDERICK DICKENS	Cob..Mr. AUGUSTUS EGG
Wellbred ....Mr. T. J. THOMPSON	Brainworm.................... ....Mr. MARK LEMON
Master Stephen....... ....Mr. DOUGLAS JERROLD	Dame Kitely .. ..Miss EMMELINE MONTAGUE
Master Matthew............ ....Mr. JOHN LEECH	Mistress Bridget ....Mrs. A. WIGAN
Justice Clement....................Mr. DUDLEY COSTELLO	Tib, Cob's Wife ....Mrs. CAULFIELD
Downright ....Mr. FRANK STONE	&c., &c.
Captain Bobadil. ....Mr. CHARLES DICKENS	

PREVIOUS TO THE PERFORMANCES AN ADDRESS, WRITTEN FOR THE OCCASION BY SIR EDWARD
BULWER LYTTON, WILL BE DELIVERED BY MR. JOHN FORSTER.

After the Comedy, Mr. Poole's Interlude of

TURNING THE TABLES.

Mr. Knibbs ....Mr. GEORGE CRUIKSHANK	Jack Humphries........ ....Mr. G. H. LEWES
Jeremiah Bumps ....Mr. CHARLES DICKENS	Miss Knibbs...........(with a song)..............Miss ROMER
Edgar de Courcy ....Mr. DUDLEY COSTELLO	Betty Larkins ....Mrs. A. WIGAN
Thornton ....Mr. T. J. THOMPSON	Mrs. Humphries ....Mrs. CAULFIELD

To conclude with Mr. Peake's Farce of

COMFORTABLE LODGINGS:
OR, PARIS IN 1750.

Captain Bonassus...... ....(an old French officer)............... ....Mr. FRANK STONE
Bombardier Barbillard..............(his companion)......... ....Mr. JOHN LEECH
Vincent Dorville ....(Lover of Antoinette) .... Mr. AUGUSTUS DICKENS
Sir Hippington Miff........................(an English Traveller).... ....Mr. CHARLES DICKENS
Rigmarole ....(Sir Hippington's Valet)........Mr. MARK LEMON
Roue .... (a broken Lieutenant) ....Mr. GEORGE CRUIKSHANK
Monsieur de Cachet ....(Intendant of Police)....................Mr. G. H. LEWES
Gregory .... (Servant to Bonassus) ....Mr. AUGUSTUS EGG
Antoinette............. ....(with a Song)......... ....Miss ROMER
Madame Pelagie ....(Sister to Bonassus).......................................Mrs. CAULFIELD

The Band will Perform,

BEFORE THE COMEDY ....**THE OVERTURE TO WILLIAM TELL,**
BEFORE THE INTERLUDE...............**THE OVERTURE TO THE BARBER OF SEVILLE;**
BEFORE THE FARCE ....**THE OVERTURE TO GUY MANNERING,**

No Money will be received on the Night of Performance except at the Gallery Door.

The Performances to commence at Seven o'clock EXACTLY, *by which time it is particularly requested that the whole of the audience may be seated.*, and that all should appear in full dress.

NOTICE.—The Address, written by Sir Edward Bulwer Lytton and spoken by Mr. John Forster, will be published in Liverpool, on Wednesday Evening, by Mr. Webb. It will also be on sale at the Theatre, after the first act of the Comedy. Price One Shilling. The Profits in aid of the Benefit.

1847 Poster

THEATRE ROYAL.

UNDER THE MANAGEMENT OF MR. HENRY COLEMAN.

ATTRACTIVE BILL FOR SATURDAY EVENING!

TWO NEW DRAMAS.

MR. JAMES BROWNE,
MR. BAKER,
AND
MRS. CHARLES SELBY.

The new Farce of MISERIES OF HUMAN LIFE.

This Evening, SATURDAY, July 31, 1847,

Will be performed the Romantic Melo-Drama, in three acts, of

WARDOCK KENNILLSON;

OR, THE WILD WOMAN OF THE VILLAGE.

Richard Lister	Mr. MORTIMER
Justice Ramble	Mr. FITZROY
Farmer Lister	Mr. J. M. ANDERSON
William	Mr. HARALD
Barleycorn	Mr. J. WALTON
Thomas	Mr. JACKSON
Murdock Kennillson	Mrs. J. WALTON
Alice	Mrs. SUTER	Manse	Miss DOUGLAS

After which, the laughable Farce of

THE MISERIES OF HUMAN LIFE.

Mr. Ally Croaker	Mr. BAKER
Mr. Mildmay	Mr. FITZROY
Mrs. Courtney	Mrs. SUTER
Margaret	Mrs. CHARLES SELBY

To conclude with a Scottish Legendary Melo-drama, founded on Sir Walter Scott's Novel, entitled

THE TWO DROVERS;

OR, THE HIGHLANDER'S VENGEANCE.

Squire Triby	(a Landholder)	Mr. HARALD
y Waakfield	(a Yorkshire Drover)	Mr. J. WALTON
Robin M'Combich	(a Highland Drover)	Mr. MORTIMER
Hugh Morrison	(a Lowlander)	Mr. WILLIS
Ralph Heskett	(a Publican)	Mr. JONES
Fleece Bumpkin	(Mr. Selby's Steward)	Mr. JACKSON
y M'Alpine	(Keeper of a Public-house)	Mr. KNOWLE
Elspat	(a Prophetess)	Mrs. J. WALTON
Martha M'Alpine	(Betrothed to Robin)	Miss DOUGLAS
Mrs. Heskett		Mrs. SUTER

Highland Lads, Lasssies, Farmers, &c.

ON MONDAY EVENING, the Comedy of

EVERY ONE HAS HIS FAULT,

With the Farce of the

HANDSOME HUSBAND

of the three balconies were adorned by elegant candlestick fittings, ornamented with pendants of cut glass. Twenty four of these were spaced around the lower tier and decreasing numbers around the higher tiers. Apparently the proscenium was thought to have been too richly ornamented for there was a criticism that although beautifully executed, it did not entirely harmonise with the light, elegant decorations of the other parts of the house.

The playbill for the inaugural performance announced that - "The new Theatre Royal will be open this present Monday, 6th June 1803 when an Address, in Character written by T. Dibdin Esq., would be spoken by Thomas Knight. After which their Majesties Servants will perform the Comedy of *Speed the Plough*. To which will be added a musical entertainment called *No Song, No Supper*.

"The doors to be opened at six and the curtain to rise precisely at seven. Tickets to be had at the box office, front of the theatre, where places for the boxes may be taken from eleven 'till three o'clock. Nights of performing will be Monday, Wednesday, Friday and Saturday."

As a consequence of rebuilding the theatre, the considerable increase in weekly expenditure and the great expense of new scenery, furniture, additions to the band and the general establishment, the lessees found it necessary to make a small addition to the prices of admission as follows - boxes 4/6d, upper boxes 4/-, pit 3/- and gallery 1/6d.

The objective of making the theatre worthy of the second town in England, would appear to have been more than achieved, for an account of the opening in the *Monthly Mirror* for July 1803, pronounced it as "the most elegant, commodious, compact and most chastely proportioned building for the purpose of theatrical exhibition in the United Kingdom."

Following the death of William Thomas Lewis on 13th January 1811 his son, Thomas Denison Lewis, and a John Banks became the lessees with the original co-lessee Thomas Knight, after whose death on 4th February 1820 there was a succession of lessees during the ensuing 65 years.

The most important bearing on the fortunes of the new Theatre Royal was the loss of its monopoly of theatrical entertainment as a result of the Government Act of

1843 for regulating theatres. In order to meet the increased competition from rival theatres, the Royal was renovated, and improvements made to the seating, also the admission prices were reduced as follows - dress boxes 3/-, upper boxes 2/-, pit 1/- and gallery 6d.

Despite the fact that the press had supported the abolition of the Theatre Royal's monopoly, it then appeared unfair that they should criticise the policy of price reductions, reasoning that this would be detrimental to maintaining the standard of drama. The Theatre Royal had the unpopular distinction of being more opposed to the extension of drama than any house in England, therefore the press apparently did not take into account the necessity for price reductions to retain audiences in competition with the other theatres.

It was also necessary to introduce more popular plays such as *Josephine* or *The Fortunes of War* and *Alexander the Great* whilst continuing to attract some leading stars of the time like Fanny Kemble, Barry Sulivan and Henry Irving and in 1847 a rare stage appearance of the famous novelist Charles Dickens in the play *Every Man in his Humour*.

It transpired that the abolition of the Theatre Royal's monopoly did not have such advantageous results as had been anticipated and its objections were proved to be correct when it was found that there was not sufficient interest in drama to keep several theatres open, subsequently resulting in the the closure of lesser rivals.

Although the Royal was principally a playhouse, Italian operas were staged with great success in November 1811, but apart from a visit by the Italian Opera Company in February 1857, plays formed the entertainment, for which the patent was renewed in 1859 for 21 years to William Robert Copeland, who was the last to hold it. The sequence of plays was thereafter broken only on 21st August 1871 when the house opened as the Theatre Royal Palace of Varieties under the direction of Harry de Frece, but at the end of that year variety ceased and the building was styled as the Theatre Royal & Opera House.

In 1862 both the Theatre Royal and

it's principal competitor, the Royal Amphitheatre, had been the subject of criticism in the Liverpool newspaper *The Porcupine* in which it was stated that they were shabby when compared to the magnificence of St. George's Hall, opened in 1852 and the William Brown library of 1860. It was further claimed that the entrances to both theatres were narrow, dirty and badly lit and at the Theatre Royal the chairs in the dress circle were hard and far too small. To make matters worse, the approach to the theatres by dank reeking streets with the stench of market refuse was even dangerous to health.

The outlook for the Theatre Royal became even more unfavourable in 1866 for that year saw the opening of two new theatres, the Star Music Hall, opposite in Williamson Square and the Alexandra Theatre in Lime Street. Whilst they prospered the once elegant Theatre Royal was being remorselessly strangled by the competition of its new rivals. The patent expired in 1880 and was not renewed, which marked the end of the Royal's once powerful influence in the presentation of drama in the year when Liverpool became a city. By January 1880

the last theatrical lessee Mr. John Chute had taken over and remained in charge until 1884. The shapely interior was then converted for use as a circus, which opened on 24th November of that year by Mr. Alfred Eugene Godolphin Cooke. Despite the considerable cost of the alterations, the venture failed and in August 1885 the building was for sale by auction, but the highest bid being only £7,000 it was not then sold. Although the Theatre Royal had survived and remained open during all the crises caused by the War of American Independence and the French and Napoleonic Wars, it was ironic that it should fall victim to the long period of freedom from major war which followed.

The use as a circus was continued by John Sanger & Sons, and it was opened for the last time on 24th December 1887 as Sanger's Hippodrome. Presenting the largest equestrian company in Europe, evening performances were at 7.30pm, also matinees on Wednesday and Saturday at 2.30pm, to which admission was 6d, 1/-, 2/. - and 3/-. This too was a short term venture, after which the building was purchased by Liverpool Corporation for £23,000 and in

1890 it was acquired by a limited company and converted for use as a cold store, its final use before demolition in 1970. At that time the only reminder of past glories was the imposing facade, then painted black, upon which was mounted the large sign in gold letters of the Union Cold Storage Co. Ltd.

1824 THE PANTHEON/LIVER THEATRE, Church Street

Although Church Street was paved in 1760, it was not until the beginning of the nineteenth century that shops and houses were erected, but the parapet was not flagged until 1816. A few years later in the 1820s one of the new buildings to be opened was styled as The Dominion of Fancy which had an interior adorned with mirrors and ornate decorations and used for balls, parties and the exhibition of Dioramas. This was the first of such exhibitions in Liverpool, and can be best described as a system of scenic representation by which paintings were viewed from a distance through a large opening illuminated by direct and reflected light with coloured blinds to produce light and shade.

In the early 1820s it was the generally expressed wish of the citizens for a second theatre in Liverpool, but the obstacle was that a second patent would have been an infringement of the patent rights for the production of plays, secured to the Theatre Royal by Act of Parliament in 1771.

There would probably have been no second theatre for a considerable time but for a Mr. John Scott, who about 1824 moved to Liverpool from London, where he had sold a theatre for £25,000. Despite the Theatre Royal's patent rights, Mr. Scott decided to convert the Dominion of Fancy into a theatre, and this was located on the first floor above some shops extending to Brooks Alley. The entrances to the boxes and the pit were in Church Street and at that end of the tastefully decorated auditorium, which accommodated between 800 and 1,000 people, a small stage was constructed. A good company for the enactment of stage plays was engaged, new scenery provided, and the opening c1825 was as the Pantheon Theatre, no doubt chosen by Mr. Scott since he had acted at the London theatre of that name. Originally the Pantheon was open only from November to Easter and not being exclusively used for the presentation of drama, as early as 1829 accommodated the waxworks figures of Madame Tussaud.

Towards the end of 1829 the theatre came under the control of Richard Malone Raymond and W.J. Hammond, who had been popular performers at the Theatre Royal. They changed the name to the Liver Theatre, and appropriately placed over the main entrance a handsome, carved and gilded representation of the fabulous bird from which Liverpool is thought to have been named. Under the successful management of Messrs. Raymond and Hammond the Liver gained popularity in the presentation of dramatic plays. In 1836 they came into dispute with the management of the Theatre Royal due to their arranging to stage a play which had already been performed at the Royal and had not been licensed by the Lord Chamberlain for re-presentation. The management of the Royal then decided to use their powers to stop the production, by Mr. Raymond, by that time in sole control of the Liver, Mr. Hammond having dissolved his partnership, petitioned the Government for the granting of the same rights and privileges enjoyed by the Royal. The petition had the support of the Corporation and was signed by 11,000 people, but there was naturally an objection to it by Mr. Clarke, the lessee of the Royal, who stated that a second patent house in the town would result in financial ruin for him. In support of this he claimed that despite the appearance of first class performers from the Metropolitan theatres, even in the present circumstances, receipts were not sufficiently large to cover expenses, and in the circumstances of competition from a second theatre, Mr. Clarke announced his intention to terminate his lease of the Theatre Royal in January 1842.

The petition for licensing the Liver was granted on 1st September 1841, but after it was forwarded to the Home Office,

Mr. Raymond was informed on 4th October 1841 that the Secretary of State did not propose to recommend the grant of letters patent for a second theatre in Liverpool.

In an attempt to meet the heavy commitments he had entered into in view of the granting of the licence, Mr Raymond appealed to the Secretary of State in January 1843 to consider his unfortunate position regarding the prosecution of his theatre by the proprietors of the Theatre Royal. Their repressive attitude towards Mr. Raymond brought about the passing in 1843 of the Act of Regulating Theatres, which resulted in the patent theatres losing all their ancient privileges, except that they were exempt from a yearly renewal of the licence.

The Liver Theatre was the first in England to be licensed under the new Act, whereby since that time the theatres of this country have been licensed. In emulation of the Theatre Royal the name was changed to the Royal Liver for the opening by Mr. Raymond on 9th October 1843, when the principal attraction, *The Rivals*, was supported by plays entitled *Cramond Brig* and *High Life Below Stairs*.

Mr. Raymond's first dramatic season under the new licensing laws terminated on 16th March 1844, after which the presentation of plays was continued during frequent changes of management. Originally the plays reached a reasonably high standard. Phelps, the great tragedian, played a season there in 1843 which included Shakespeare, but by 1848 the Liver had sunk so low as a dramatic theatre that conjurors were engaged. Although in April 1849 an operatic season was inaugurated, the last manager of the theatre, Mr. Robert Edgar, held the position for only a short time as by 11th May 1850 the building had been converted into the Liver Drapery Establishment, remaining in this use until the early 1900s it became a music store by a Mr. William Lea who constructed two additional shops in the premises.

1825
THE SANS PAREIL THEATRE,
Great Charlotte Street

A large circular wooden building known as the New Rotunda originally occupied the site of this theatre, 18 Great Charlotte Street, which had been erected by a Mr. Marshall and opened in June 1825 as Marshall's Moving Panorama exhibiting the Bay and City of Naples. Later in that year the interior was converted into a theatre, which was opened by a Mr. W.J. Holloway as the Sans Pareil (without equal). Its success is indicated by the fact that in the following year Mr. Holloway carried out improvements to make it larger and more comfortable. The auditorium then had a pit and a gallery to which admission was set at 3d and 6d for the two performances daily at 5.30pm and 7.00pm.

The theatre was considered to be the home of good acting as a rule rather than the exception, and at Christmas excellent pantomimes were produced. The Sans Pareil continued to prosper during the next five years and in 1831 Mr. Holloway decided on the building of a new theatre, during which time the company performed in a spacious hall in Castle Street.

The New Sans Pareil Theatre opened on Monday 26th November 1832 with plays entitled *Eugene Aram, Damon and Pythias* and *Wallace, the Hero of Scotland*. The seating was then arranged in boxes at 1/6d, pit at 1/- and the gallery at 6d. Due to the growing demand for new theatres in Liverpool, the Sans Pareil was again successful, and together with the Pantheon/Liver Theatre and the Hop in Dale Street, they vied with the Olympic Circus in breaking down the monopoly of the Theatre Royal.

During its 11 years of life, the Sans Pareil, also the Pantheon/Liver and other theatres of a still lower description were referred to in a Home Office report on juvenile delinquency following a Government inquiry. It was alleged that an incredibly large number of children frequented the

theatres where they fell into bad company and committed thefts of articles from members of the audience.

The closure of the theatre in 1843 was apparently unconnected with the aforementioned problem. Mr. Holloway announced in the *Liverpool Mercury* of 7th April that after fifteen successful seasons he was to relinquish the building since it was to be demolished due to street improvements.

1826
COOKE'S NEW CIRCUS/THE-ROYAL AMPHITHEATRE/ROYAL COURT THEATRE,
Queen's Square/Great Charlotte Street

The Amphitheatre was originally opened as a circus by Mr. John Cooke in order to continue the great success which he had achieved at his Olympic Circus in Christian Street. The site chosen was the piece of land now occupied by the Royal Court Theatre in Roe Street, formerly Queen's Square at the junction with Great Charlotte Street. The laying of the foundation stone on 27th November 1825 was followed by the construction of the building under the supervision of a Mr. Armistead. The main frontage with entrances was then in Great Charlotte Street, whereas in

the new plan as the Royal Court in 1881 and the re-built theatre of 1938, the main entrance was sited in Queen's Square, the present Roe Street along which extended the length of the building.

The original facade was most imposing with a facing of stucco work resembling white stone. It comprised three storeys of which the lower one was rusticated, the wide recessed divisions giving the appearance of separate stone sections. The centre portion of the facade projected forward and included the entrance to the best seats in the boxes, with, on either side a tall iron standard supporting a glass-shaded gas light fitting. The lower part of the elevation also included several tall arched windows and at the extreme sides, entrances to the pit and the gallery. Above this level the central section of the frontage was adorned by four Corinthian pilasters, supporting the entablature with frieze upon which was carved in the stonework - Royal Amphitheatre - and the pediment above bearing the Royal Coat of Arms.

The building, 135 feet in length and 76 feet wide had an auditorium which it was estimated would accommodate 3,000 to 4,000 people. In addition to the circus ring it featured a stage 51 feet in width, a 41 feet proscenium opening and three tiers of boxes and galleries. It was stated that the interior

presented to the eye, a prevailing mass of crimson enriched with burnished gold mouldings and ornaments. The whole being enhanced to the glow and radiance of an oriental palace by a large and splendid, movable gas chandelier suspended from the ceiling, also numerous subsidiary gas fittings spaced around the fronts of the boxes and galleries. The passages and entrances were considered to have been well planned, and those leading to the boxes were adorned with busts, paintings and other appropriate ornaments. Proof of the fact that Mr. Cooke had considered stability to be no less important than splendour, was provided in the report of three eminent surveyors, appointed by the Mayor to examine the strength of the building.

Considering that the construction was in the first half of the 19th century and taking into account the vast size of the building, it might be considered surprising that it was at a stage sufficiently near to completion to enable the opening as Cooke's New Circus to take place on 27th February 1826. Apparently the haste to open was responsible for the fact that the theatre was then only partially decorated and in a very unfinished state, thereby bringing forth the comment in the Liverpool Mercury that when completed, the building would be a credit to the town, and a lasting monument to Mr. Cooke's persevering industry.

The circus had not long been open when John Cooke decided to present a stage play *Rob Roy* but having no licence to do this resulted in prosecution by the lessees of the Theatre Royal, who about 12 months later in 1827 again took action against Mr. Cooke to prohibit the performance of a comic opera for the benefit of Ellar, a prince among harlequins, which they claimed was an infringement of their rights and privileges.

Towards the end of 1827 Mr. Cooke ended his term as proprietor and manager, the theatre then coming under the control of lessees, Messrs. Wyatt and Farrell, who were succeeded by Andrew Ducrow, under whose lesseeship in 1840 the establishment was known as Ducrow's Royal Amphitheatre of Arts, but towards the end of that year this was shortened to Royal Amphitheatre, and often referred to as The Amphi.

During the ensuing 40 years several other lessees were in charge of the theatre, which was mainly a venue for drama, interrupted when there was a period of closure

from 27th June to 22nd August 1859 for the purpose of structural alterations including a new stage and the gallery enlarged to accommodate 1,000 persons.

The Amphitheatre had for some time been the Royal's strongest competitor, but although a greater choice in the arrangement of productions was available to the lessees of the former, due to the passing of the Theatres Act 1843, competition between the two leading theatres resulted in both lowering the standards in order to survive. This brought about some diversification in the entertainment at the Amphitheatre to include ballet and musical productions, one of which in 1849 starred Jenny Lind, the famous prima donna, known as the Swedish Nightingale.

In the early 1860 s the Amphitheatre became Liverpool's leading venue for entertainment as the fortunes of the Theatre Royal declined, several lessees followed in succession until 1880 when the sole and last lessee of the Amphitheatre prior to extensive alterations, Mr. Lindo Courtenay was given a benefit performance on 28th February 1881 when the theatre closed with a performance at 7.30pm of the celebrated comedy in four acts by Mr. Frank Harvey entitled *John Jasper's Wife*. This was suc-

ceeded by *A Musical Melange* and to conclude, the first act of *Robert Macaire*. It was reported that the performance was played to a lively audience in the pit and the gallery, between which there was a continuous fusillade of popping ginger beer corks and showers of nut shells!

The theatre was then for sale by auction and bought by Sir David Radcliffe for £20,000, after which the interior was entirely gutted and re-built to the designs of Mr. Henry Sumners, an eminent local architect. It was announced that the whole building would be thoroughly well ventilated, beautifully decorated, and lighted, also fitted with every modern appliance necessary for the working of a first class theatre. In the reconstructed auditorium, a new and improved proscenium opening was erected with two tiers of boxes on either side and two additional tiers at either side at the rear of the horseshoe-shaped dress circle. Also the stalls were furnished with moveable seats designed by the architect. It accommodated, with the pit stalls, 450 people, whilst the pit and gallery each contained 800 seats. Each part of the house had its individual refreshment bar, ladies and gentlemens cloakrooms, toilets etc. Externally as before, the pit and gallery were approached by two separate entrances in Great Charlotte Street, but for patrons of the higher priced seats in the boxes, dress circle and stalls, a new entrance was constructed to the right-hand side of the long elevation to Queen's Square. The entrance was covered by the principal section of the full length verandah, on the facia of which was displayed in white opaque glass, the new name - Royal Court Theatre. External lighting was by gas light within globular shades, suspended by metal brackets, spaced along the verandah.

With its new name, the Royal Court, the theatre was re-opened by the sole lessee and manager, Captain R.H. Bainbridge, also lessee of the Theatre Royal, Manchester, on Saturday 10th September 1881 when the inaugural performance consisted of the new and original opera in three acts entitled *The Lancashire Witches* or *King Jamie's Frolic*, performed by the resident opera and dramatic company selected from the principle

London and provincial theatres. Admission to the private boxes was £2/2/- and £1/1/-. The orchestra stalls, dress circle and pit stalls were 5/-, 4/- and 2/6d respectively. For those wishing to avoid the crush, the pit and gallery doors were open from 6.30pm to 7.15pm when patrons were admitted for 2/- and 1/-.

David Radcliffe to the Carl Rosa Opera Company for £40,000. The new proprietor opened the theatre on 31st March 1884 with a revival of T*he Ticket of Leave Man*, and the Christmas of that year saw the appearance of the Carl Rosa Opera Company, which for more than 12 years subsequently provided the Christmas attraction.

3rd August 1896, then opening with Mrs. Bernard Beere's company in *Masks and Faces*. The Christmas pantomime from 23rd December of that year, *Cinderella* was wonderful and a great success, each performance playing to enthusiastic and delighted audiences.

But the success was abruptly, even though in the circumstances, for a surprising short time, interrupted when the theatre was seriously damaged by fire in the early hours of Saturday 9th January 1897. *The Liverpool Review* reported the incident as follows - *"It has been said that unforeseen misfortune is apt to bring on madness. This assertion emanating from whatever source has been absolutely falsified in the case of Robert Arthur, whose handsome theatre was very seriously damaged by fire in the early hours of last Saturday morning, 9th January. It was only on the Wednesday before Christmas that a wonderful and successful pantomime of Cinderella was produced on the Court boards, and subsequently up to the time of the disaster, each performance was full with the greatest enthusiasm by a crowded and delighted audience. Then came the crush, an irretrievable crash, as many people thought it would be. In the course of last Saturday's conflagration, the roof of the theatre was destroyed, the gallery was nearly destroyed and the circle, pit stalls and boxes were greatly damaged. Hundred of pounds worth of costumes and properties were ruined."*

Between the hours of 4.00am and 6.00am 2,000,000 gallons of water were poured into the building and the firemen received great credit for the fact that the theatre was not absolutely gutted, but on the contrary, so much of it was saved. At first it did appear however that the odds were against a speedy re-opening. The lessee, Robert Arthur was soon at the scene, consulting with the building surveyor with regard to the best course of action. With remarkable resource and spirit, he quickly arranged for the removal from the theatre of all the charred items by the cartload and for the quickest possible repairs to the damage, both in regard to the building and everything relative to the pantomime, with offers

At the end of the March 1884 Captain Bainbridge severed his connection with the theatre, which was then sold by Sir

Mr. Robert Arthur, who was to have a long and successful association with the theatre, became the lessee and manager on

PROGRAMME

"ALL·THE·WORLD'S·A·STAGE"

Royal Court Theatre

And Opera House, Liverpool.

MANAGING DIRECTOR **Mr. ROBERT ARTHUR**

Royal Court Theatre, Liverpool;

Theatre Royal, Newcastle-on-Tyne;

Theatre Royal, Nottingham.

Her Majesty's Theatre, Dundee

Her Majesty's Theatre, Aberdeen.

Any Cause of Complaint should at once be referred to the Acting Manager.

Mr. ARTHUR will be glad to receive Suggestions (by letter) from Visitors.

CLOAK ROOMS FREE. NO GRATUITIES.

Acting Manager - . . . . - Mr. ARTHUR LAWRENCE
Musical Director- . . . . - Mr. J. O. SHEPHERD.

FRASER & WHITE, PRINTERS.

of help from the entire company.

In view of the scale of the damage, the seemingly impossible was achieved, for in the incredibly short time of 5 days and nights it was possible to re-open the theatre on 14th January with the pantomime, again packed to capacity by a delighted audience. *Cinderella* was presented until 6th March, to be followed on 8th March by the Royal Carl Rosa Opera Company performing a different opera each evening.

During the 26 years from 1898, the highly esteemed manager of the Royal Court was Mr. Arthur Lawrence, who at the age of nineteen had made his first stage appearance at the Prince of Wales Theatre, Clayton Square. In those days, near to the turn of the century, when nobody had heard of motor cars or cinemas, theatre-going was an ingrained social habit, both a duty and a festival and the Royal Court was a rendezvous de luxe for lovers of drama and opera in all their various guises. Everyone who was anyone could be encountered in the foyer, and carriages at 10.30pm provided transport for the more affluent patrons. It was not necessary to travel to London to see the stars of the theatrical firmament, for they practically all came on tour to the Court, where were welcomed in turn - Sir Henry Irving, Ellen Terry, Beerbohm Tree, Wilson Barrett, Lewis Weller and George Alexander etc. It was also the favourite provincial theatre of producer George Edwardes, who frequently came to Liverpool with his companies, for which the Court held five attendance records. It is a little known fact that Sir Henry Irving died on the eve of a visit to the theatre, he passed away at Bradford after his performance in *Becket* in October 1905, and not only was it a Friday night, but it was also the thirteenth! All arrangements had been completed for his appearance on the following Monday at the Court, the advertising was out, and heavy advance bookings had been registered. At such short notice it was only with great difficulty that Mr. Lawrence filled the tragic blank, eventually securing the services of the well known actor, Weedon Grossmith. A good example of the old theatrical proverb - *Actors may come and actor may go, even great actors, but the play must go on*

ROYAL COURT THEATRE, QUEEN-SQUARE, LIVERPOOL.

Sole Lessee and Manager.....Mr. R. B. BAINBRIDGE.
Lessee of the Theatre Royal, Manchester.

Important Theatre, the rebuilding of which (upon of the old popular Amphitheatre) is now approaching completion, has been erected by Mr. David Radcliffe, of front the Designs and under the immediate ice of Mr. H. Sumners, Architect, also of ....ced to Boxes, Stalls, Dress Circle, and Pit is now by a spacious covered Canopy from Queen-s, the approach being by a handsome Staircase.

he Stage Opening has been erected upon a new and improved principle, and has Two Tiers of Boxes on either side, on each tier : the Dress Circle and Stalls will be seated with Moveable Seats, designed by the Architect, and will accommodate, with the Pit Stalls, 450 persons, and have their own Refreshment Bar, Ladies' and Gentlemen's Cloak-rooms, Lavatories, &c.

The Pit and Gallery are approached by Two Separate Entrances fronting into Great Charlotte-street, and will each accommodate sitting 800 persons. Both Pit and Gallery are provided with their own Refreshment Bars, Lavatories, &c.

The whole structure will be thoroughly Well Ventilated, Beautifully Decorated, Lighted, and entirely Refurnished and Fitted with every modern Appliance necessary for the working of a First-class Theatre.

THIS NEW AND MAGNIFICENT THEATRE WILL OPEN SATURDAY, SEPTEMBER 10, 1881.

Production of the NEW AND ORIGINAL OPERA, THE LANCASHIRE WITCHES; Or, KING JAMIE'S FROLIC! Written by R. T. GUNTON. The Music by F. STANISLAUS. Special Engagement of MADAME CAVE-ASHTON. Prima Donna of the Crystal and Alexandra Opera, MISS ALICE COOK. Of the Alexandra Palace Opera. MADLLE. MARIANI. MISS CONSTANCE LOSEBY, Prima Donna, Alhambra and Gaiety Theatre, London. MR. HENRY WALSHAM. Primo Tenor of Her Majesty's and Carl Rosa Opera Companies. MR. W. H. WOODFIELD, Primo Tenor, Alhambra Theatre, London. MR. T. F. DOYLE, Prince of Wales and Alexandra Theatres, Liverpool; Theatres Royal and Princes, Manchester.

forever!

During his time at the Royal Court, Arthur Lawrence produced 20 pantomimes with such great stars of the day as George Robey, John Humphries, Walter Groves, Harry Lauder, Little Tich, the Three Sisters Levy and the Poluski Brothers. Although George Robey was considered to be the best pantomime comedian, the greatest success was *Aladdin* in 1906, which starred Hetty King, Happy Fanny Fields, Malcolm Scott and the famous comedian Harry Tate. Average takings were only just under £2,000 per week, which was remarkable considering that the theatre grossed no more than £275 at full capacity.

The Royal Court continued to be one of Liverpool's leading theatres during the Great War 1914-18, and in this period a notable attraction, presented for the first time in 1915 was the musical comedy *Tonight's The Night*. A Grossmith and Laurillard enterprise, it followed on to the Gaiety Theatre, London. The cast included in a

small part, Leslie Henson, who in later years was to achieve fame as a star of musical comedy and films.

The success of the theatre began to wane in in the 1920s for in addition to the cinemas in the city centre the re-built Empire Theatre opened in 1925, provided strong competition with many top class musical productions. But the proprietors of the Court, still the Robert Arthur Theatre Company, experienced more difficult times from 1929 when the cinemas were gradually equipped for sound films, known as the talkies.

In the early thirties under the management of Messrs. Howard & Wyndham, a merger of theatre interests was formed with Moss Empires, proprietors of the Empire. This was stated to be for the purpose of supplying to both theatres, bigger and better drama and finding the right play for the right theatre. There was an opinion, however that this would mean the loss of competition, and Liverpool playgoers therefore being offered not what they wanted, but those plays which the theatre controllers decided to present. It was hoped nevertheless that this would result in a return to the former glory of the Royal Court, which had not fully recovered from a disastrous policy of twice nightly stock company plays. It was therefore a severe blow to theatregoers when without advance announcement, the theatre closed on 22nd April 1933, especially since this took place at the end of a week during which it had been packed to accommodate the large crowds who attended to see the excellent play *Service* brilliantly presented by Percy Marmont, Ann Casson and a particularly competent company. The suddenness of the decision to close is indicated by the fact that the local press advertisements and playbills announced the attraction for the following week - *Le Chauve Souris*.

In July 1933, the Royal Court was acquired by a new company, the Royal Court Theatre Co. (Liverpool) Ltd., of which the chairman was Mr. Maurice Voss of Voss Motors Ltd., with Alderman J. C. Cross and Mr. H. Buxton as joint managing directors. It was announced that although internal arrangements at the theatre would not be

theatre had been emptied of the largest audience it had held since turning over the variety. Lesss than 25 minutes after Alderman Cross and other officials had left the theatre, Miss Norah Baird, an employee at the Victoria Hotel opposite, noticed the glare of fire above the theatre roof. She gave the alarm and a few minutes after the arrival of the firebrigade, the roof collapsed, the interior of the building was converted into a shambles of twisted girders, fallen masonry and seared woodwork. The circular-shaped auditorium had acted as a funnel for the flames which shot high in the air. The flames licked unavailingly at the safety curtain and due to its strength , the artists' property was saved. With the reinforce-

altered, before the re-opening therewould be a spectacular change to the facade, which had become drab and dingy.

A new page in the history of the Royal Court was turned on August Bank Holiday 1933 when it went over to variety which raised the comment that because of the change there was probably much turning over in graves! But such macabre rustlings were inaudible in the theatre, which was crowded with a vastly enthusiastic audience. The management engaged as musical director, Mr. Frank Stokes, formerly stage director at the London Palladium, who led one of the best known orchestras in the theatrical profession. Top of the bill, for the first time in Liverpool was Geraldo and his orchestra from the Savoy Hotel, London. A high spot among the supporting artists was the incredibly fast tap dancing of Richard Castle and Rosalind Wade, whist further amazing foot and limb work came from Max Wall, a dancer of exceptional ability. The bill also included Keith Wilbur and Billy Matchett etc. The performances were twice nightly at 6.35pm and 8.50pm with admission prices 6d to 3/-.

But as if in the the nature of a punishment by the Muses of Comedy and Tragedy upon the management who had dared to turn the historic theatre into a music hall, disaster struck at aprroximately 11.30pm on Saturday 22nd September 1933, after the

PLAN OF DRESS CIRCLE SEATS

PLEASE EXAMINE THE DATE & NUMBER OF YOUR TICKET.
KINDLY KEEP THIS ENVELOPE AND HAND IT TO THE ATTENDANT.

ment of four additional fire engines, it was two hours before the blaze was bought under control. But from the street it looked as though nothing had happened, the untouched and newly painted exterior giving no hint of the devastation within.

Demolition was not completed until March 1938 and it was announced by Mr. A. Stewart Cruikshank of the Robert Arthur Theatre Co., that plans had been drawn up for the early re-building of the theatre, which would be run with the same policy of stage plays as at their theatres in Manchester, Newcastle, Glasgow and Edinburgh, but variety would be excluded.

1832
ZOOLOGICAL
GARDENS THEATRE,
West Derby Road

A long forgotten theatre which was situated in the beautifully laid out Zoological Gardens and whilst it is not possible to state when it was first established, this was probably soon after the gardens were first opened by a Mr. Atkins in May 1832.

It is recorded that for many years the theatre was in public favour and its small stage presented Vaudeville and Farces, interspered with singing and dancing by a number of talented performers. With the exceptions of the gallery, where a small change was made, admission to the performances was free.

The theatre is thought to have closed at about the same time as the gardens in 1865.

1842
THE PRINCE OF
WALES THEATRE,
Vauxhall Road

Although the name Prince of Wales in normally associated with the theatre and later the cinema in Clayton Square, nearly 20 years before the historic *Little House in The Square* was opened, a theatre of the same name was opened in 1842. The only recorded information available is that the theatre was closed soon after its opening due to representations made to the Mayor concerning the nature of the performances. An investigation took place and found the allegations were completly unfounded , the theatre being well managed and the entertainment above reproach. The Mayor then granted to the proprietor full permission to reopen, after which the inaugural performance consisted of the plays, *Vasha, the Slave Queen,* and *Nicholas Nickleby.*

This is another long forgotten theatre, about which no further details appear to exist.

1846
THE HOP,
Dale Street

This unusually named theatre, sometimes called the Penny Hop situated at 140 Dale Street, was originally styled as The Mechanical Exhibition Rooms which was opened c1830 by a Mr. John Caloe as a Theatre of the Arts, where could be seen mechanical working models of The Storm at Sea, The Bay of Naples and The Eruption of Vesuvius. In addition there was a representation of The Birth of Venus, whilst a beautifully modelled figure told the fortunes of ladies and gentlemen. Other entertainments included negro minstrels, legerdemain and marionette performances, for which the wax works figures were all made in the workshop behind the stage.

The place was converted into the Hop Theatre in August 1846 and a small but good working company was assembled for the presentation of real legitimate drama and generally included a few professional actors wishing to fill in time between engagements.

Mr. Caloe continued to run the theatre until its final closure in 1860 during which time he claimed that nothing of a degrading or immoral nature was presented, the plays and exhibitions being of a highly intellectual and instructive nature, affording entertainment to thousands of patrons at a cheap rate.

THE PENNY HOP,
Hood Street

This was apparently Liverpool's poorest theatre, the interior consisting of a spacious room fitted up in the crudest fasion with a small stage at one end and the seats on an incined floor. Plays were performed during the 1840's to the poorest people of the city, many without shoes or stockings.

No further information is availabe concerning this little known theatre.

1847
THE PARTHENON
ASSEMBLY ROOMS/
PARTHENON MUSIC HALL/
THEATRE MODERNE,
Great Charlotte Street

The building was erected in the early 1840's and opened as the Parthenon Assembly Room, described as new and spacious. They were at first used for various kinds of entertainment of which first advertised was a ball on 25th February 1845. In the following August, the building was open to the public as Bianchi's Wax Works and exactly a year later it came under the direction of the proprietor, Mr. John G. Stoll, who in order to stimulate buisness, supplemented the wax works show with live performers, announcing that an unrivalled company of dancing and vocal talent was engaged nightly. There was no admission charge, the entertainment then being provided from the sale of refreshments, the hall was then named the Parthenon Music Salon and in 1850 the Parthenon Rooms. The earliest known play bill announced on 20th May 1850 - Models of Art, Tableaux Vivants and Poses Plastique for which the doors were opened at 6.30pm for the performance at 7.00pm of one continued routine of Tableaux and Songs with Mr. John Reed, the old favourite comic vocalist and Miss M. Baxter, the celebrated singer from the London and Glasgow concerts.

The proprietor announced the complete success of this truly classic exhibition, stating that it would be his constant study to produce for the future a succession of novelties which would merit a continuation of the patronage with which his establishment since its opening had been honoured.

Later known as the Parthenon Music Hall it continued under the direction of J.G. Stoll for a considerable time and after his death in 1880, his wife took over the running of the theatre. A year later her son, Oswald, who in the 1890's was to form his own circuit of music halls left school aged 14 to assist his mother in the running of the Parthenon. It was described as a beer and sawdust

hall, where the prices were so low that the most expensive were those at a shilling in the boxes at either side of the stage, where

the people were locked in to prevent the more unruly among them getting on to the stage. In front of each row of seats was a rack for the purpose of holding glasses of beer!

In his training as a music hall manager, Oswald Stoll was mainly concerned with the clerical side of the business, whilst his brother Roderick was identified with the front of the house. In his negotiations for artists, Oswald Stoll had only his stepfather's record of payments to guide him but he nevertheless showed wonderful astuteness in his management of the hall and was soon considered an able caterer. The Parthenon stage was graced by many well known stars of the variety firmament, the Leno family with young Master Dan, Marie Loftus, Harry Lauder, Bransby Williams and the most popular favourite of all, Vesta Tilley, a young male impersonator for whom Oswald Stoll wrote several songs. It was considered that but for Vesta Tilley there might have been no circuit of Stoll music halls, for it was her engagement to his rival, a handsome young Jew, Walter de Frece, one of her many suitors, which decided Oswald to move as far away from Liverpool as possible. At that time the de Freces were also business rivals for apart from the agency in the Roscoe Arcade, they ran the Gaiety Theatre in Camden Street and the Theatre Royal as lessees.

In 1890, then aged 23, Oswald Stoll moved to Cardiff to make his first bid for fame and fortune by re-opening Levino's Music Hall, which became the first of his many successful Empires, and commencing the Stoll Tour of Music Halls.

The Parthenon continued as a music hall with a Mr. George Atkinson as manager and in the latter part of the 1890s it came under the control of a syndicate, of which the managing director was a Captain W. Siater. The manager, then Edwin W. Smith subsequently became the proprietor, and early in 1904 the hall was re-constructed internally and made more commodious. In 1906 Edwin Smith severed his connections with the theatre and following a period of closure the Parthenon re-opened on 20th November 1906, advertising in the *Liverpool Echo* - Moving Pictures and

Vaudeville Company. A week later vaudeville had been superseded by the moving pictures, of which were to be shown - *Miles and Miles of the latest Events* also, for the first time, the great American sensation *The Life of a Detective*. It was described as the family entertainment of the city, not to be missed, and performances were at 7.00pm and 9.00pm, also a matinee on Tuesday.

Ownership of the Parthenon at that time cannot be confirmed, but one source of information states that it was run by the Pathe Freres' Cinemas Ltd., film renters of 32 Paradise Street. It was later renamed the Theatre Moderne where the entertainment consisted of motion pictures and two artists, who sang a song with an appropriately illustrated slide on the screen   if the projector broke down.

This short term venture terminated in 1908 when the building was acquired by Messrs. Henochsberg and Ellis and converted into a clothing establishment. Later it became a Reece's cafe, which survived through the 1930s, but in 1940 the building was destroyed by enemy action in World War II.

1850
ROYAL COLOSSEUM THEATRE/ SAUNDER'S THEATRE OF VARIETIES/ CITY THEATRE OF VARIETIES/NEW GRAND THEATRE & OPERA HOUSE/ QUEEN'S THEATRE/ KELLY'S THEATRE,
Paradise Street

This early location of 'live' entertainment is notable for the great variety of names bestowed upon it by the many owners and lessees during the 66 years in which it catered for patrons of both drama and variety. With more changes of name than any other theatre in the Liverpool area, this was a conversion from a Unitarian Chapel, erected late in the 18th century and opened for public worship in 1791. It was octagnal in shape with one of the sides allocated for the principal entrance, whilst on either side of the octogan were two windows and an attic balustrade, ornamented with vases at each angle, extending around the structure, which had a large octoganal lantern in the centre. The grounds included a graveyard, enclosed by iron railings with entry by a handsome iron gate.

The Unitarians left Paradise Street in 1849 in favour of a Gothic style edifice in Hope Street, after which the Chapel was for sale and bought privately on behalf of a Mr. Joseph Heath. The work of conversion into a theatre commenced and surprisingly, having regard to its former use, this was assisted by some of the original internal features. This was due to its spaciousness and well constructed gallery with front richly inlaid and veneered with beautiful woods. The pews of the chapel were brought into use for seating accommodation.

Opened in 1850 by Joseph Heath as the Royal Colosseum Theatre & Music Hall, it was no doubt the first to be constructed with twin auditoria, for whilst the theatre presented what were described as full blooded dramatic plays for a patronage of mariners from the Wapping and other nearby docks, there was also in the portion of the building fronting on to Paradise Street, offering the alternative of variety performances. These entertainments continued for several years, being well suited to the taste of those for whom Mr. Heath catered.

When the Colly, as it was familiarly called, first opened there was the unusual arrangement that, in order to enter the theatre, patrons had to pass through the graveyard, which partly encircled the building. This led to an increasing belief amongst the youthful members of the patronage, that some spirit, doomed to walk the night, haunted the vicinity of the theatre. But whether or not this was true, the fact remained that prior to the removal of the remains for re-internment elsewhere, there was never any shortage of a skull during a performance of *Hamlet*. These were easily obtained, the artists' dressing room, below the stage, formerly having been a grave vault, the artist had only to put his hand through an opening in the thin dividing wall, to seize hold of the grisly relic, as did Hamlet!

After acquiring a considerable amount of property in the neighbourhood, Joseph Heath died in the early 1870s leaving his properties including the theatre to his son, Thomas Theodore Heath, under whose control the Royal Colosseum continued to be successful. The theatre came under the control of the first of a number of lessees in 1875 when Mr. C.H. Duval opened on 27th September with the play *The Ticket of Leave Man*. Within three years another lessee, Mr. Jacob Goodman had taken over, and had the misfortune that his tenancy was marred by a panic among the audience on 11th October 1878 when a portion of the ceiling fell into the pit and resulted in a false alarm of fire, and the loss of 37 lives in addition to many injured. The theatre was then closed for a year, during which time, alterations included the replacement of the wooden pillars supporting the gallery by others of iron. According to an official source, at that time there was accommodation for 3,000 people, thereby indicating that possibly the principal alteration was to a single auditiorium, although this has not been recorded.

Styled as the Royal Colosseum Temperance Concert Hall, the re-opening took place in December 1879, beginning a series of concerts inaugurated by a committee of local gentlemen under the presidency of a Mr. William Simpson. This attempt to revive the fortunes of the old theatre did not prove successful and in 1880 Mr. Dan Saunders, formerly manager of the Star Music Hall, took over and re-opened on 26th April with the name Saunders Theatre of Varieties.

Throughout the 1880s a succession of lessees resulted in further changes of name. Mr. Saunders, being succeeded in 1881 by a Mr. P.Wilcocks, who renamed it the City Theatre of Varieties, as it was known until a further period of closure in 1884, although with a period in between when drama was presented by different lessees.

After renovation in 1884 it was re-opened by Mr. W. Potter with another change of name to the Grand Theatre of Varieties. In the following year, Messrs. Wilmot and Roach of the Grand Theatre in London were the lessees. Later, under the control of Mr. Roach as the sole lessee and manager, it continued as the Grand Theatre until another closure on 26th February 1894.

The theatre then came under the control of two grandsons of the original founder, Joseph Heath, and a second attempt was made to revive its past glories with so great a scheme of refurbishment and redecoration that internally and externally it was hardly recognisable. The reopening on Whit Monday, 3rd June 1895 was as a dramatic house styled as the New Grand Theatre and Opera House. This was run by

Messrs. John Edgar and Albert Heath for two years, then purchased by Messrs. Elliston and Machin for about £18,000, remaining in their hands until July 1901 when a lessee, Mr. T. Morton Powell reopened on August Bank Holiday of that year, also holding the position of manager until closing in December 1903.

The greater part of the building was demolished early in 1904, the only remaining parts of the old building being the frontage and portions of the side walls. The new facade of the Queen's Theatre, as it was to be known, included many stonework architectural features in classical style. A verandah bearing the theatre name was fitted above the central main entrance, in the form of an archway adorned by the Royal Coat of Arms, and flanked on either side by three arched windows. The upper part of the three storey frontage included niches with statues of famous theatrical personalities of the time, fluted pilasters and numerous windows, of which, in the centre, the largest

of these was set above a stone balustrade, and flanked on either side by columns supporting an entablature, upon which statues supported a frieze bearing the theatre name.

Passing through the main entrance way, one entered the imposing vestibule leading into the entrance hall with ornate ceiling, mahogany walls and doors, flooring of Italian mosaic and oxidized silver electrical fittings, an up-to-date feature at that time being that the theatre was lighted throughout by electricity. The plans provided for commodious refreshment rooms and close to the stage, nine dressing rooms and two star dressing rooms, but none below as in the old theatre. In the new auditorium seating 2,000 people, the ceiling, the proscenium and the fronts of the boxes, circle and gallery were decorated in fibrous plaster work of unique design in tints of cream and gold picked out with crimson. The stalls and the horseshoe-shaped circle were fitted with tip-up seats in crimson plush and

at either side of the 27 feet by 26 feet proscenium opening, four boxes each accommodated six persons.

The Queen's Theatre was opened on August Bank Holiday 1904 by lessees, Messrs. Carson and Granville of the company known as Granville Theatres Ltd., of which Mr. Frederick Granville was the popular managing director. The opening presentation, a drama entitled *Bigamy* was well attended and indicated every hope for the success of the new venture.

After only a few years the theatre was taken over by its last proprietor, Alderman William Wallace Kelly, who could have been Lord Mayor of Liverpool had he so wished, and was described as the grandest of theatrical grand old men, who always wore a silk hat and a flower in his button-hole. His Merseyside enterprises began in 1897, when he became the proprietor of the old Theatre Royal in Birkenhead, which he brought to life again and after leasing the Birkenhead Metropole, he acquired the Queen's, then declining in popularity, giving it a new lease of life as Kelly's Theatre. He was the pioneer in bringing to it the Irish Players from the famous Abbey Theatre in Dublin, also presenting long operatic seasons at low prices.

Alderman Kelly also assisted the movement which led to the establishment in 1911 of the Liverpool Repertory Company, and led by Miss Darragh and Basil Dean they gave a six week's experimental season at Kelly's Theatre, which proved so successful that they moved to a permanent home at the Star Theatre, re-opening it on 11th November as the Liverpool Repertory Theatre. It appears therefore that Alderman Kelly, unselfishly, in the interests of drama provided his own competition.

With a history of providing every type of entertainment through the years, and after presenting drama for about two years, Kelly's Theatre made a final change to variety performances before closing on 31st October 1916.

The building was sold to the then well established grocers and restaurant proprietors, Cooper's Ltd., who premises fronted on to Church Street, for use as their

PROGRAMME

warehouse, but this ended in May 1941 when the building was destroyed in an air raid.

1850
THE QUEEN'S HALL/ BIJOU THEATRE & OPERA HOUSE, Bold Street

The building at number 65 Bold Street was originally erected as an assembly hall for religious services known as Dr. Thom's Chapel, which about the early 1850s was converted into an elegantly fitted theatre with a small stage. Named the Queen's Hall and later the Queen's Operetta House, it was a popular venue for musical and a dancing entertainments, including in 1865, Charles Christy's Minstrels who had also appeared at the Theatre Variete, Lime Street.

The proprietor and manager in 1866, Mr. J.S. Lofthouse, also controlled the Oxford Music Hall in Lime Street and the Cambridge at the corner of Warwick Street and Mill Street. He sold the Bold Street theatre after only two years and during the

ensuing fifteeen years there were quite frequent changes of proprietors and lessees. The proprietor in 1880, a Mr. Booker granted a 14 years lease to Messrs. Bell, Woolrich and Brown, a period noteworthy for the fact that on 3rd May the theatre was opened wtih the lengthy title of The Bijou Theatre and Drawing Room Opera House, in which the opening performance was given by the Liverpool Amateur Operatic Society.

The success of the theatre after a short time resulted in improvements being carried out, at a cost of £2,000 to the lessees and £1,000 to the prorietor. Later, Mr. Bell became the sole lessee at a rental of £310 per annum and in 1882 acquired an adjoining house for the purpose of improving the entrance and providing increasing space for a new waiting room, ladies cloak and retiring rooms, refreshment bars, a wider gallery staircase and improved access to Back Bold Street.

The cost of this work to Mr. Bell was about £500 and the additional   space increased the yearly rental to £420.

It was therefore unfortunate that before the end of the year of such marked improvements, the theatre was closed on 26th December1882 due to the collapse of a wall at the rear of the building in Back

Bold Street. There, in an excavation 32 feet below, the Cheshire Lines Railway opened out from a tunnel close to the theatre, and the formation of the ground at this part necessitated that in the building of the cutting there should be a retaining wall for the safety of Back Bold Street. It was reported that in his action against the railway company, Mr. Bell was awarded damaged to the amount of £500.

The theatre survived for another ten years under the control of other lessees and managers, then closing during the early 1890s for conversion into shops.

1852
THE ROYAL PARK THEATRE, Park Street

Although the building had originally been constructed as a store for the sale of manure, this first playhouse in the south end of Liverpool was described as an attractive place of entertainment after the conversion to a theatre.   It was opened on 27th September 1852 by Robert Edgar, the husband of the clever tragedienne, Alice Marriott, with all the fittings and scenery which he had purchased on the closure of the Liver Theatre in Church Street.

There was a change of control in October 1859 when a Mr. John Campbell became the lessee, and with stage plays as the principle entertainment and a pantomime at Christmas, the theatre was open until the early 1900s when it was converted into a warehouse.

1859
THE THEATRE VARIETE/ ST. JAMES'S HALL/THE TIVOLI PALACE OF VARIETIES, Lime Street

Following the demolition of several dilapidated houses in 1845, Lime Street was widened and on part of the site, the Teutonic

Hall was erected to the plans of the architect, Edward Starkie Tuton, although despite its name there was nothing Teutonic in its origins. After a decade in use as a public hall, the interior was converted into two separate areas, the ground floor being occupied by Allsopp's New Crystal Palace Waxworks, whilst the upper floor, styled as the Teutonic Upper Hall exhibited Hamilton's Dioramas. In 1859 this was converted into the Theatre Variete under the ownership of Messrs. Wilson and Montague, who in April 1863 presented the first of the Charles Christy Minstrel Shows, the forerunner of what in later years was to become the most popular and longest surviving entertainment at the hall. A change to stage plays in 1865 introduced famous actors such as Brinsley Sheridan, Charles Wyndham, and the second Liverpool appearance of Henry Irving. Continuing under the same ownership, in the spring of 1868, the theatre was re-named the St. James's Hall and Operetta House, the entertainment consisting of plays, ballets and operas. From 31st October 1870 and for over 25 years this was Liverpool's home of minstrels. Its destiny was guided by the famous Sam Hague, whose troup of performers numbering about 40, organised by him in Macon, Georgia, U.S.A. were stated to be "the only genuine darkie troup in the world."

After four and half years of great success, Sam Hague was the victim of a disaster on 2nd May 1875 when the theatre and all of its property, which he had purchased for the sum of £30,000 were destroyed by fire. It was thought that the fire had broken out backstage in the Green Room, or in one of the dressing rooms and then spread into the auditorium. Although this became a charred mass of ruins, the flames were prevented from spreading to the wax works below, or to the adjoining County Court. Unfortunately for Mr. Hague, the hall was only partially insured for £5,000 and the fittings etc for £4,000. Another great loss was the famous organ, owned by a gentlemen known as Herr Schalkenbach. This had taken a considerable time to build and was insured for £900, an amount far below its true value.

The Mayor of Liverpool, Lieutenant Colonel Steble and a number of influential gentlemen then organised with great success, a benefit performance for Mr. Hague and his minstrels at the Amphitheatre. The troup later went on tour, Sam Hague then dividing his attention between them and the erection of his new St. James's Hall on the first floor of the building. At ground level five shops and an oyster bar replaced the former wax works, and at the extreme right of the frontage, the main entrance led into the much enlarged vestibule, 12 feet wide, with access to the oyster bar on the left and 20 feet in length to the wider staircase. This led up to a first floor area with stairway on the left to the first gallery and entrance to the rear right-hand side of the stalls. The first gallery had a straight front facing the stage, straight extensions along either side, and three boxes on the right. At the rear of this floor a stairway was ascended to the rear of the second gallery, which extended over about 20 feet with a straight front. With dimensions of 80ft by 35ft this was about the same size as the old hall, but with a larger seating capacity of about 1,000 due to the addition of a new gallery. Surmounting the ornate 25ft wide proscenium, an American eagle stood out in bold relief from the centre of a large wreath of oak leaves, against a background representing in gold, the rays of the sun, whilst at either side were two figures emblematical of Mirth and Dancing.

Almost exactly one year after the fire, the new St. James's Hall was opened on 1st May 1876 and for a score of years, Sam Hague and his minstrels were successful in maintaining the tradition of St. James's Hall as Liverpool's leading venue for this type of entertainment.

Early in 1896 the St. James's Hall was acquired by Mr. James Kiernan, who several years previously had taken over the Paddington and Park Palace theates of variety and was the fountain head of a new venture to convert the time honoured St. James's Hall into the Tivoli Palace of Varieties. The mere mention of James Kiernan at that time in connection with an undertaking of this kind, was then a guarantee of its success, having regard to his past efforts in providing places of entertainment in several areas of Liverpool.

In February 1896, an army of workmen under various contractors were busily employed day and night with hammer, chisel, trowel and brush in the task of altering, reconstructing, improving and beautifying the old home of Negro Minstrels. In fact after completion, it was considered that so great had been the change internally, that Sam Hague, upon his next visit would be unlikely to recognise the place.

Externally on the right-hand side of the frontage to Lime Street, the main entrance, in the form of a beautiful Grecian portico, with design in white and gold, was surmounted by a magnificent coloured glass arch, with superb rainbow illumination over the entrance doors. Brilliantly lighted by elecricity and gas, the beautiful decorations of the foyer were in relief with colour and gold ornamentation, whilst the ceiling with high relief decorations was in pale cream and gold. A feature of this area was the half circular pay box, surmounted by a rich tent-like hood, beyond which was the grand

staircase to the stalls, pit and gallery. Midway up the staircase a fine decorative arch was constructed, with its beautiful proportions and bright artistic embellishments representing an architectural feature of itself. On the staircase, decorated in gold, were mounted six electric arc lights and candelabra illuminated by incandescent bulbs in crystal globes to shed a brilliant light over the whole area. At the head of the staircase the first floor lounge, as those of the other parts of the house, was decorated by palms, plants and flowers and furnished by bamboo settees and chairs.

Stepping into the auditorium, illuminated throughout by electric light, was compared to encountering a veritable fairy tale scene, a striking and most pleasurable lightness of tone having been effected by a harmonious combination of colours, pale warm yellows with cream, heightened by a profusion of gold in the relief ornamentation. Here also the use of mirrors was conspicuous and, in harmony with the graceful architecture, sixteen panels in Pompeyian style were symbolical of music, dancing and poetry etc. The radiance and beauty of the hall was enhanced by hundreds of electric globes set in three massive bronze chandeliers. Flanked on either side by artistically arranged palms and plants, the stage was adorned by a beautiful tableau curtain of peacock blue plush with primrose drapery and the proscenium was enriched by relief ornamentations in pale cream and gold with luscious effect. Presentation of the entertainment was improved by the provision of new scenery and up-to-date gas, lime and other effects.

Amid all this splendour, the comfort of the audience received consideration with tip-up seats being fitted throughout upon a floor covering in the stalls and pit of a handsome carpet of unique Brussels deisgn, whilst choice linoleum was laid in the balcony and cheaper parts of the house. The best seats, of the oval back type were upholstered in peacock blue plush, and the cheaper seats in American leather, whilst the boxes and the circle were a revelation in luxury and comfort. Above this, the gallery was improved to allow all patrons an unobstructed view of the stage.

Described as one of the most picturesque and sumptous of its kind in the United Kingdom, the Tivoli Palace of Varieties opened on 2nd March 1896, when the theatre was packed for the two performances at 7.00pm and 9.10pm. Eager crowds had awaited the opening of the doors in Lime Street and Back Lime Street, admirably regulated and held in check by a large force of police, but many were turned away, disappointed when the house filled for both performances. First and foremost among the array of talent of seventeen artistes engaged for the performance was the versatile and brilliant queen of comediennes, Marie Lloyd, who had been booked by Mr. Kiernan at a fabulous salary and music was by an orchestra of twenty picked musicians. As manager of the Tivoli under Mr. Kiernan was Mr. John Donald, a person of considerable experience in the position who was responsible for the general running of the theatre and the staff of twenty two attendants.

The popular prices were; private boxes 10/6d, single seats 5/- and 8/-, orchestra stalls 1/6d and 1/-, pit stalls 1/- and 6d, gallery 3d.

However, the venture was to be short lived for on the occasion of the second anniversary, marked by a variety performance and a Grand Fashion Night on 28th April 1898 it was announced that this was to be the last night but two of entertainment in the old building, for so many years until recently, well known as the St. James's Hall, for on Saturday 30th April it was to close for rebuilding. First exhibited on 18th May 1896 as an added attraction to the 'live' entertainment, the cinematograph pictures illustrative of a Phantom Ride were reported as a wonderful added attraction.

James Kiernan was praised for his proposed enterprise of building a new theatre at such large expenditure, but this did not materialise and the building remained unused until 1906 when Walter de Frece, husband of Vesta Tilley, and well known theatrical entrepreneur, became managing director of the South of England Hippodrome Ltd, turned his attention to the building of his first hall in the north of England. On the site of the old Tivoli the

new theatre was constructed by Messrs. Brown & Sons, contractors of Liverpool and Salford, to the plans of Bertie Crewe, the well known designer of theatres, including the Liverpool Hippodrome.

Whilst no details of the new theatre appear to exist, it can be confirmed that the frontage of the building was similar to that of the Palais de Luxe cinema prior to the post war modernisation. As previously, the quite long frontage was adjacent to the length of the building. The main entrance was at the extreme right and spaced along were the exits from the various parts of the theatre. These were surmounted by a substantial iron and glass canopy with forward extentions at either end, with shaded electric light fittings, the two adjacent to the main entrance being large lanterns. The upper part of the frontage was relieved by several pairs of pilasters and panels, three stone arches projected above the coping, and at the extreme right was a square tower.

Internally the planning differed from that of the old theatre in that the stalls floor was below ground level and reached by stairways from the left-hand side of the foyer. In this area the entrances gave direct access to the dress circle, which had an extension along either side with exits to street level, whilst above was the gallery in the rather narrow auditorium, which had a total seating capacity of about 1,500. The local press reported that all had been done to make the interior attractive and comfortable, the decorations and upholstery forming a pleasing blend of bright colouring.

On Saturday, 8th December 1906, Vesta Tilley laid the commemoration stone of the new theatre and this was preserved in the basement of the building during its 50 years as the Palais de Luxe cinema. On the occasion of the Grand Opening on Monday 10th December, the New Tivoli Palace of Varieties was stated to be the most beautiful vaudeville theatre in the provinces, with entertainment of the highest order to be found in the variety world. Top of the bill, making her last appearance prior to her American tour, was the famous male impersonator, Vesta Victoria. Joining the ranks of the two houses a night variety theatres,

the performances were at 6.30pm and 9.00pm and a matinee every Thursday. Admission was at 10/6d to the private boxes, stalls 1/6d (first three rows 2/-), grand circle 1/-, pit 6d and gallery 3d.

Walter de Frece, managing director of the company, Liverpool Theatres of Varieties Ltd., controlled the running of the Tivoli in conjunction with the Palace, Manchester, the Palace, Belfast, also the Liverpool Paddington and Park Palace theatres. From the latter he transferred the manager, James Marks to the Tivoli as resident manager.

The anticipation of success following the re-building of the Tivoli did not materialise, apparently by reason of its close proximity to Moss and Stoll's Empire Theatre where variety was also presented. Towards the end of 1907, in an attempt to improve attendances at the Tivoli, cinematograph pictures replaced variety as the top of the bill attraction. These were arranged by the Weisker Brothers, film exhibitors from St. Helens, who about that time converted several failing music halls into cinemas. With considerably lower admissions prices, these being only 1/- stalls, 6d circle, 4d pit and 2d gallery, the Tivoli remained open with cine-variety until 28th March 1908, after which it was closed for nearly 8 months until leased together with the Park Palace by Jasper Redfern, a Sheffield electrician turned film showman after successful connections with the Sheffield Central Hall and the Grand Theatre, Manchester.

Concurrently with the Park Palace, and re-renamed the Grand Tivoli, Mr. Redfern's opening performances were on 21st December 1908 with Great Pictures and Class Vaudeville presented twice nightly at 6.50pm and 9.00pm. Pictures with the Bioscope were supported by a variety bill, headed by Lila Dunbar, the celebrated Tyrolean mimic artiste with music by the orchestra led by Mr. W.A. Hollis, the first in Livepool to play in accompaniment to silent films. Jasper Redfern continued with similar entertainment until 30th June 1909. Then for the first time the hall became the Palais de Luxe cinema, with cinematograph entertainment again by the Weisker Brothers

who advertised the finest of its kind in the United Kingdom with comedy, drama and sport films accompanied by a high class orchestra. Patrons were advised - Come when you like and stay as long as you like, at peformances continuous from 3.30pm to 10.30pm. Admission was 6d stalls, 1/- grand circle, 4d pit and gallery 3d and tea was served free of charge between 4.30pm and 6.00pm to patrons of the 6d and 1/- seats.

Sole control by the lessees, the Weisker Brothers, ceased c1911 when the Palais de Luxe Cinema Company was formed to take it over, with directorate including Frederick Weisker, one of the former lessees, and Alderman W.W. Kelly, previously associated with the 'live' theatre.

The Palais de Luxe was a cinema for over 50 years, since c1920 controlled by its last owner, the North Western cinema circuit. It was closed for about one month due to bomb damage in May 1941 and for about 18 months in June 1951 after a serious fire, which was followed by considerable modernisation, internally and externally. Finally closing at a time of decreasing cinema attendances, on 24th October 1959. The building was later demolished and the site re-developed with shops.

1861
THE PRINCE OF WALES THEATRE, Clayton Square

The site of this theatre was originally occupied by Clayton House, built early in the 18th century, it became the home of Miss Clayton, whose father William Clayton was a Liverpool MP during separate periods between 1698 and 1714. It was considered that the house had the prettiest and most productive gardens in Liverpool and following the laying out of Clayton Square about 1770 other houses were converted for use as shops and offices. Clayton House was later converted into Clayton Hall, which was used for concerts, and where later a good organ was installed and inaugurated by Dr. Wesley on 23rd January 1854.

The reconstruction of the hall as the Prince of Wales Theatre was the result of a chance visit in December 1859 by a young man, Mr. Alexander Henderson, who had recently embarked from Australia. Being unable to to concentrate on the entertainment, Mr. Henderson's interest was diverted to the squarish hall with a small gallery at the rear. The idea then occurred to him of taking a lease on the building and reconstructing it to form an attractive little theatre. Without delay Mr. Henderson secured from the proprietor a lease with the option to purchase, but due to the fact that the present lease had six months to run before the building could be made available to him, Mr. Henderson returned to Australia, arriving back after six months to take possession and arrange for his scheme of improvements. The reconstruction of the hall at considerable cost was completed in time for the opening as the Prince of Wales Theatre on Thursday evening, 26th December 1861, when the principal item was a comedy-drama item, *The Maid with the Milking Pail* followed by a burlesque entitled *Miss Emily O'Connor*.

It was considered that no truer or pleasing description of the theatre could be desired than that obtained in a novel *Dorrie* by William Edwards Tirebuck, wherein he stated that in this very cosy, comfortable little house, the stage seemed part of the orchestra, the orchestra a part of the stalls, the stalls a part of the pit, the opposite boxes on familiar terms with each other, the dress circle a friendly continuation of the boxes, and the gallery like a cap of liberty and fraternity capping them all.

But nevertheless a more detailed description of the theatre is as follows - The three storey frontage was spanned for the greater part by an iron canopy with deep facia of glass bearing the theatre name and supported along the front by iron columns. The upper part of the frontage incorporated six tall first floor windows with iron railings in front and above, six square windows of the second floor, surmounted by an almost full width gable. Access to the theatre was

---

Prince of Wales Theatre.

LAST WEEKS OF
North American Photo Co.

Starring Engagement of
Boswell's Miniature Circus,
Educated Ponies, Donkeys and Dogs,
Comical Clowns.

Mdlle. Luminare,
The Beautiful Fire Dancer,
from the Palace Theatre, London.

Miss Ada Twybell,
AND
Grand VARIETY PROGRAMME

Every Evening at 8.
Matinees—Monday, Wednesday and Saturday at 3.
Prices—3s., 2s. 1s. 6d., 1s., and 6d.
Box Office open 11 to 3.

---

by several small entrance ways, each with a pair of panelled doors which led into separate foyers for admission to the various parts of the house. In the auditorium, 55ft in length and 35ft wide, most of the seats on the ground floor were described as the pit except for the three rows of higher priced seats nearest to the orchestra. Above, the curved fronted dress circle and the gallery with straight side extensions extended to a minimum depth of 35ft in the centre of the auditorium, the former terminating with boxes adjacent to the proscenium. A large crush room at the left-hand side of the first floor gave direct access to the dress circle and the boxes, whilst stairways in the centre and right-hand side rose to the dress circle saloon with entrance to the gallery. Several dressing rooms and a property room were provided in the basement and access to the

area below the stage. In the following year, 1862, the building was enlarged, incorporating part of the neighbouring Brunswick Hotel, and a new entrance and crush hall were provided in Cases Street. It was acknowledged that Alexander Henderson had the gift of doing the right thing at the right time and his plan was to have a first rate stock company chiefly consisting of rising young players, content with modest salaries and providing good support to the stars, who rapidly found at the Prince of Wales financial advantage in addition to public appreciation.

Mr. Henderson's first five years in charge of the theatre were successful. Noteworthy during this time was the beginning of a new and important phase in the career of the actor, Henry Irving, who during his appearances at the Prince of Wales rapidly improved in his art, commencing there his third engagement in December 1865.

Alexander Henderson left to take over the management of the new Prince of Wales Theatre and Opera House, Lime Street in 1866, the Clayton Square theatre then being taken over by Mr. William Brough who opened it as the Theatre of Varieties on 26th December 1866 with *King Arthur* or *Knights of the Round Table*.

During the period of fifteen years from 1869 there were about six changes of lessees until Alexander Henderson returned to take control in April 1884. Plans for internal and external improvements were then drawn up and promptly put in hand. The frontage was given increased height above the gable, pilasters supported a stone balustrade and a large ornamental model of the Prince of Wales feathers was fitted within the pediment.

By the spring of 1885 Alexander Henderson had finally severed his connections with the theatre and for the first time a lady, namely Fanny Josephs took over and was succeeded after her death in 1890 by her husband. In 1896 the last proprietor before a period of closure was H.B. Nelson who, it was reported ran the theatre in first class style until 1st June 1901 when the final performance was of a stage play, *The Private Secretary* at 8.00pm, preceded by *Box and Cox* by Gilbert and Sullivan at

PRINCE OF WALES THEATRE,

CLAYTON SQUARE, LIVERPOOL.

Sole Proprietor and Manager ... ... Mr. GEORGE C. CLEAVER.
Director of Animated Pictures ... ... Mr. RALPH PRINGLE.

MONDAY NEXT, the 25th instant,

And every Evening during the Week,

GRAND RE-OPENING

BY THE

North American - - - Animated Photo. Co.

GENERAL BULLER'S FAREWELL TO THE ARMY.
ARRIVAL of the NEW PRINCE and PRINCESS OF WALES.
GRAND SERIES OF ANIMATED PICTURES.

☛ LIVING LIVERPOOL, ☚
A DAILY RECORD OF LIVERPOOL LIFE.

LORD MAYOR'S SUNDAY IN LIVERPOOL.

New Animated Pictures of the Boer and China Wars.

MILITARY BAND 30.. PERFORMERS.

The Home of Novelty, Mirth, and Laughter.

10,000---ANIMATED PICTURES---10,000

Depicting THE WORLD'S HISTORY Day by Day.

SPECIAL ENGAGEMENT OF . .

Mr. LINDON TRAVERS, FELLOW OF THE ROYAL GEOGRAPHICAL SOCIETY,

Just Returned from South Africa,

Who will give his Pictorial Recital, "How Buller won the Victoria Cross."

CONGREGATION LEAVING ST. LUKE'S CHURCH.

MONDAY NEXT, 25th inst., Illustrated Recital, "THE VILLAGE BLACKSMITH," by the

MINSTER VOCAL QUARTETTE

(Messrs. Chas. Aspinall, Tom Barlow, W. S. Redmond, and Fred. Owen).

MATINEES on Wednesdays and Saturdays at 3.

POPULAR PRICES—Dress Circle, 3s.; Circle and Stalls, 2s.; Pit Stalls, 1s. 6d.; Pit, 1s.; Gallery, 6d.
Nightly at 8; Doors open at 7-30. Early doors open at 7,—6d. extra; Pit and Gallery 3d. extra.
Box Office open from 11 to 3. Children Half-price to all parts.

Printed on English-made Paper by Trades' Union Labour, for the "Liverpool Review" Printing and Publishing Co., 64, Victoria Street, Liverpool,
by The New Century Printing Co. (Liverpool) Ltd., 59, South Castle Street, Liverpool, SATURDAY, NOVEMBER 23rd, 1901.

7.30pm.

The theatre was then put up for auction, but no sale was affected, the highest price offered being only £13,000, despite the fact that prospective buyers were advised that during the thirteen weeks run of the previous Christmas pantomime *Cinderella* in the 1,300 seat auditorium, receipts had amounted to over £17,000.

In September 1901 the theatre was purchased by Mr. George C. Cleaver who reopened it on 25th November with the new attraction of animated pictures by the North American Animated Photo Company. Under the direction of Mr. Ralph Pringle was presented a grand series of 10,000 animated pictures including those of the Boer and Chinese wars. There was also Living Liverpool, a daily record of local life and The World's History day by day. Mr. Linden Travers, fellow of the Royal Geographical Society was specially engaged and music was provided by a military band with thirty musicians. The evening peformance commenced at 8.00pm and matinees were on Wednesdays and Saturdays at 3.00pm. The popular prices were - dress circle 3/-, circle and stalls 2/-, pit stalls 1/6d and gallery 6d. Although the doors were opened at 7.30pm there was also early doors admission at 7.00pm when patrons could avoid the rush on payment of an extra 3d or 6d.

The local press reported that the animated pictures together with the musical entertainment had proved most successful and Pringle's Pictures, as they were known, continued to draw large audiences for several weeks, continually being brought up to date with new films of local events supported by an excellent variety show.

The Christmas 1901 attraction was advertised as the latest thing in cinematography, *Little Red Riding Hood,* a pantomime in moving pictures, which it was reported gave delight, particularly to the children and enormous business was recorded. After its run in January 1902 the pictures continued together with refined vaudeville and a full orchestra, this type of entertainment ending on 20th January after which the theatre was closed for over seven months.

On 1st September 1902 a new era

dawned for The Little House in the Square when it was reopened as a high class theatre under the management of Messrs. C. St. John Denton and George Blunt for the presentation of the latest London successes - comedies, musical plays and light operas. However, the opening attraction was the dramatic play, *All in the Family* followed by a new farce, *Off the Rank.*

The benefit performance on 7th November 1902 to Messrs. Denton and Blunt by the Strollers Dramatic Society's presentation of a one act comedy, *Cut Off with a Shilling* and *School for Scandal* was considered a fitting final performance prior to closure for alterations. After these the theatre reopened on 24th December with the pantomime *Puss in Boots* with great success, the Prince of Wales pantomimes having been famous throughout the years for their elegance and fun.

After Messrs. Denton and Blunt retired from the management of the theatre in 1904 they were succeeded by lessee and manager John H. French, the last lessee to acquire it before final closure. Opened on 24th December, the Grand Juvenile Pantomime *Little Red Riding Hood* was stated to be played by the cleverest cast of children in the world, to which there was an evening show at 7.30pm and matinees on Monday, Wednesday and Saturday at 2.00pm. This was followed on 13th February 1905 by Mr. H. Barr's company presenting *Cinderella* which ran until Saturday 25th February 1905 when the theatre closed.

The building was not used until 1910 when it became the auction rooms of George Turner & sons and was demolished in July 1912.

The 1860s were noteable for the opening of several music halls in the Liverpool area. Most of these were closed before the end of the last century and little is known about these long-forgotten halls. For the record they are listed below t ogether with the available information.

This impressively-named entertainment was presented in what was merely a structure of wood and canvas in Crosshall Street, which opened on 26th December 1862 with the pantomime Harlequin and Tim Bobbin or The Lancashire Witches. It was later known as Myer's Circus and in 1864 as the American Opera House, but there is no record of the final closure.

1861 THE CASINO/PRINCESS THEATRE, Bevington Hill

This building at 23 Bevington Hill was originally intended for use as a market, but in the early 1860s it was renamed the Princess Theatre. Later opened by Dan Lowrey it was given the unusual title - The Nightingale Palace of Music & Recreation. The prices of admission, which included refreshments, were 3d, 4d and 6d. In 1870 it was the Victoria Music Hall and later in the 1870s when the proprietor was Mr. H. Ambrose there was a change of name to the Casino Temperance Hall. Later John Tudor bestowed upon it his own name, styling it Tudor's Varieties, and after further changes of proprietor and name the building closed as a place of entertainment in the early 1900s. For many years it was used for commercial purposes.

THE LIVER MUSIC HALL, Mersey Street

Located at 46 Mersey Street this was also known at Ceda's Music Hall, which during the late 1860s was under the management of Signor Antonio Devoto.

THE ROYAL ALHAMBRA MUSIC HALL, Derby Road, Bootle

This hall in Derby Road, Bootle was built and opened by Mr. John Hill. With popular prices it was well attended for many years by the residents of the north end of Liverpool and, of course, Bootle. The auditorium was situated on the first floor, the ground floor area being allocated for an hotel, an American Bowling Alley and a concert room. The theatre had a pit on the lower floor and a gallery above, to which entrance was from Derby Road and Esk Street respectively. Closed c1888.

THE EAGLE MUSIC HALL, Old Hall Street

Opened during the 1860s at 73 Old Hall Street, it was managed by a Mr. R. Ford, and later by a Mr. Levine. Remaining on the exterior for at least forty years was the old insignia of the eagle.

1865 THE NEW ROYAL THEATRE /THE ALHAMBRA MUSIC HALL Manchester Street

This place of entertainment at 46 Manchester Street was situated on the first floor above several shops, with entrance by a flight of stone steps. The theatre had a pit, a small gallery and stage boxes to which admission prices ranged from 3d to 2/6d. It was opened in January 1865 as the New Royal Theatre with a full dramatic company. For some time stage plays were presented but with a change to pantomime at Christmas.

Later under the direction of Harry de Frece, the establishment was known as the Alhambra Music Hall, the first in the provinces to introduce a policy of two performances nightly, which proved popular. In 1876 Mr de Frece left to take up the management of the Gaiety Theatre in Camden Street and was then succeeded by Joseph Travers. It was then known as the Alhambra Temperance Music Hall until closure about 1879.

THE CAMBRIDGE MUSIC HALL, Warwick Street/Mill Street

Another first-floor theatre, this was situated at the corner of Warwick Street and Mill Street with the main entrance in the former. The auditorium held about 900 people, with a balcony which curved around the sides to the proscenium. It was described as prettily decorated, the walls and the ceiling displaying artistic pictures depicting science, music, morning, night and the seasons.

The Cambridge was opened by Mr. J.S. Lofthouse on 4th July 1865, when the variety bill included Mr. and Mrs. Leno, the Brothers Leno and the Lancashire Clog,

Boot and Pump Dancers. There was originally one performance nightly but later, under the management of Mr. B. Walker, two performances were given. Closed as a music hall about 1878 it became known as Templar's Hall, a place for religious purposes during the first decade of the present century.

THE OXFORD MUSIC HALL. Lime Street

Situated in Lime Street, it was opened about 1866 by the proprietor of the Cambridge, Mr. S.S. Lofthouse, who also ran the Queen's Hall in Bold Street, plus a hall in Dublin. By this time Mr. Lofthouse had a good reputation for engaging popular performers and later opened a variety agency in London. Following the success of his enterprises he met with a premature death by a chill. Mr. B. Walker of Cambridge then took over the management.

THE CONSTELLATION MUSIC HALL Whitechapel

Number 74 Whitechapel, at the corner of Charles Street, was the location of this music hall, opened by the proprietor, Jonas Cohen, under the management of Harry de Frece on 24th December 1866, when the doors opened at 6.30pm for the performance at 7pm exactly. From the Charles Street entrance admission to the stalls and side gallery was 6d and to the body of the hall with a refreshment ticket, it was also 6d. From the Whitechapel entrance admission to the back gallery was 3d with a refreshment ticket. Refreshments were of the alcoholic type, consisting of wines and spirits, ale and porter, and for patrons wishing to have a meal, steaks and chops were available.

1866
NEW PRINCE OF WALES THEATRE/ROYAL ALEXANDRA THEATRE/ EMPIRE THEATRE,
Lime Street

Erected on the site of the present Empire Theatre, the original building dates back to 1866 when the foundation stone was laid by Mdlle. Titiens of the Italian Opera Company, after which the construction took place during the ensuing nine months by Messrs. Jones & Co of Liverpool to the plans of the architect, Mr. Edward Solomons. The lower storey of the facade comprised a series of five arches with pilasters and surmounted by carved capitals in which the lion heads served for ventilation, for which purpose the mouths were pierced. Although two of the arches were later occupied by shops they were originally all entrances. The arch to the left was the entrance to the carriage drive, that to the right was the entrance to the pit and the circle, whilst the central archways were for patrons of the stalls and the dress circle. Extending above the line of five first floor windows pilasters extended up to the frieze, surmounted by the coping and the enriched stone balustrade. Another feature of the frontage was the carved heads in stone of Shakespeare, Schiller, Molier, Beethoven and Rossini, emblematical of drama and music.

Although at that time Liverpool's largest theatre it was only about three-quarters of the size of the present Empire, and of an entirely different plan, featuring three horseshoe shaped balconies. The lower of these bordered on three sides the approximately half circular stalls area, terminated, as the circle above, with two elegantly curtained boxes. Six cast iron pillars spaced around supported the balconies and above, suspended from the ceiling, the dominant feature was the enormous artistically-designed chandelier illuminated by numerous gas-light fittings. Additional lighting was provided by gas with fittings spaced around the balcony fronts etc., whilst on stage, this was the first theatre in Britain to use the Defries fish-tailed gas burners. In front of this,

the proscenium was in the form of a high arch.

The original proprietors included a number of well known merchants and commercial people. A banker, Benjamin Heywood Jones was the chairman of directors, which included William Langton, son of the first manager of the Bank of Liverpool, and for a time chairman of the Dock Board. The theatre was opened by Alexander Henderson, proprietor of the Prince of Wales, Clayton Square, who obtained a lease on the property and moved to take over the new theatre. With the name The New Prince of Wales Theatre & Opera House, the grand opening was on 15th October 1866 when *Faust* was presented by the Italian Opera Company with Mlle. Titiens who, nine months previously, had laid the foundation stone, in the part of Margherita.

Alexander Henderson's short term as lessee ended in 1867 when he was succeeded by H.J. Byron and in that year, on 29th July to honour the Princess of Wales,

there was a change of name to the Royal Alexandra Theatre & Opera House. The stage lighting was then improved by the installation of glass sealed, gas footlights, which had individual chimneys built into a side wall as exhaust for the fumes. There was also limelight which travelled by long rubber tubes from storage tanks manufacturing oxygen and hydrogen in the basement. To this was attributed the destruction of many theatres by fire or explosion, also the burns suffered by numerous artists, but apparently the subject theatre escaped such disasters and accidents.

The fortunes of the Alexandra were greatly helped by the fact that the proprietors were able to retain as manager, Edward Saker for a period of fifteen years until near to the time of his death in 1883. He was an accomplished actor excelling in Shakespeare's clowns and was well known for his Shakespeare revivals. During his reign, in addition to Italian operas and Christmas pantomimes, plays were frequently presented by the Alexandra stock company. Among the many famous artists who appeared was the distinguished actor Henry Irving, for the first time locally in *The Bells* and Sarah Bernhardt, in 1881 by express permission of the Lord Chamberlain in *The Lady of the Camelias.*

Edward Saker was succeeded by his wife, who apparently accepted the position of manageress for the reason that she was left with five young sons to support and she hoped to realise her husband's wish that the management of the theatre would ultimately

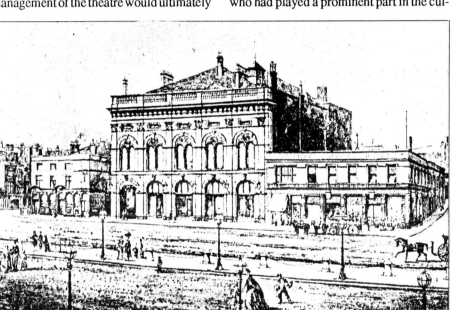

be taken up by one of his sons. But this was not to be, for Mrs. Saker retired from her position after only five years in April 1888. The Alexandra was then presenting the famous Vesta Tilley as principle boy in *The Forty Thieves*. During a farewell benefit for Mrs. Saker, Phillip Rathbone, the chairman of the Alexandra Theatre and Opera House Co. presented her with a cheque on behalf of the subscribers in recognition of her successful even though comparatively short time in charge of the theatre. In addition to the re-decoration of the theatre, the period had been innovative with a diversification of entertainment by a series of French plays, and a season of a children's comic opera company in 1886. For the first time in the provinces Boucicault's *The Jilt* was pre-

sented in 1887, and noteworthy performances were given by the Carl Rosa Opera Company in *Esmeralda* also there were return visits of Sarah Bernhardt and Henry Irving.

The Alexandra continued under new management until May 1894, and was thereafter closed until December 1894 when it was re-opened with Mr. Ellis Brammall Jnr. of the Shakespeare Theatre as manager, whose first attraction was *The Fair One with the Golden Locks*. But the company continued to suffer from financial hardship, and despite the efforts of Phillip Rathbone, who had played a prominent part in the cultural life of Liverpool, to keep the theatre open, he was forced to close it again early in 1895. The theatre then came under the ownership of a company known as Empire Theatre (Liverpool) Ltd., although retaining the name Alexandra. The managing director was John Hollingshead and despite the fact that he was referred to as Practical John, the venture did not achieve the anticipated success, and after only a few months, on 5th August, the last proprietors of the theatre as the Alexandra, the Alexandra Vaudeville Co. Ltd., directed the theatre until they relinquished control in January 1896, when the property and three shops were put up for sale by auction. It was then sold to Messrs. Moss and Thornton for the sum of £30,000. Mr. (later Sir) H.E. Moss,

who was the principle of the large syndicate, Liverpool, Leeds and Hull Empires Ltd., announced that after re-opening, the tone of the variety entertainment would be raised and of a class strictly in unison with the building, refined as it was excellent.

Throughout 1896 work proceeded on the re-construction of the interior, and improvements to the frontage under the direction of the well known architect, Frank Matcham, whose plans transformed the theatre to so great an extent as to bring forth the comment in the local press that little of the old Alexandra remained except the walls and the roof! At the highest point of the original frontage, a large stone pediment with the name Empire Theatre was introduced. At ground level one of the shops was eliminated and the other two sited at the extreme ends, the three centre openings with polished mahogany doors then forming the entrances. Above these was constructed a substantial glass and iron canopy with the theatre name in white opaque glass on the central section of the facia. This was flanked by iron standards with large glass shaded electric light fittings, the new form of lighting being installed for the first time throughout the theatre. Beyond the entrances the large and lofty grand vestibule was handsomely fitted up. All the doors, the paybox and other woodwork was in polished mahogany whilst the floor was laid in marble. The ceiling had mouldings and enrichments with centres filled in with hand paintings of exquisite design. An entirely new white marble staircase was constructed, the first flight of great width, branching off to the left and right to the grand and upper circles. The original inconvenient and winding staircases were therefore dispensed with and the space obtained added to the pit which was greatly increased in area, the curtain line being taken back from ten to twelve feet. The dress circle and the upper circle were re-arranged to improve the sight lines, but the architect could do nothing with the steep and badly arranged gallery, which was pulled down and replaced by one providing comfort and good sight lines. The greatest alteration was at the front of the auditorium where the old private boxes were cleared away, and the old proscenium wid-

ened to over forty feet. The wall face was lined with marble and ten feet behind a new proscenium was constructed with a circular, arched opening. Between the old and the new proscenium were very handsomely decorated stage boxes with canopies, whilst at the sides next to the auditorium, groups of further private boxes made a total of ten, and under the box arcades were the entrances to the orchestra stalls.

Flanked on either side by artistically arranged palms and plants, the stage was adorned by a beautiful tableaux curtain of peacock blue plush, and the proscenium was enriched by an extensive display of relief ornamentation in pale cream and gold. The walls were similarly treated, and enhanced by Pompeyian-style panels and numerous mirrors, the entire scheme of decoration was by Frank Matcham, and the wonderful radiance and beauty of the auditorium was enhanced by a blaze of light from a hundred electric globes set in three massive bronze chandeliers. The comfort of the audience also received most careful consideration from the architect, who provided lounges with settees, thick velvet carpets, and a high standard of seating in all parts of the house. There was little change to the stage and dressing rooms, but like other parts of the theatre, these were also heated by hot water pipes and radiators. Safety had not been forgotten, a fire-proof curtain dividing the stage from the auditorium was fitted.

The Grand Opening of the Empire Theatre took place on 19th December 1896 with Oscar Barrett's famous pantomime *Cinderella* by a cast of 200 performers direct from the Lyceum Theatre, London which commenced at 7.00pm. There was a full house, the audience received the production with manifestations of delight, and following its run, the first variety performance commenced on 15th February 1897.

Within three years, in December 1899 came the unification of ten existing theatre companies under Moss Empires Ltd., which it is recorded, resulted in Dick Thornton opting out of the circuit, of which Oswald Stoll was managing director until 1910.

Variety continued as the principal form of entertainment, for which the old Empire Theatre enjoyed so great a reputation during the ensuing 24 years after the opening. It is noteworthy however that although for a limited time only films were top of the bill on Monday 21st August 1911, when the management secured the exclusive rights for Liverpool to exhibit Kinemacolor. This was an invention of the English pioneer film maker, George Albert Smith in 1908, and although one of several systems using the colours of red and green, it was a commercial success into the early years of World War I. Kinemacolor was described as Nature's Look Glass, the only existing stereoscopic life motion pictures, reproducing the actual colours of nature without any artificial means of colouring. With performances daily at 6.40pm and 9.00pm, the

films were exhibited until 30th September 1911, but from 4th September augmented by a variety bill.

For those not called up to the services during World War I, 1914-18 a visit to the Empire was a pleasant even if brief release from the anxieties of war, after which the theatre continued into the 1920s, when in addition to the performances by the British National Opera Company, famous artistes to make their appearance included Jack Hulbert and Cicely Courtneidge, Ivor Novello, Fay Compton and Dame Sybil Thorndike, who played the lead in *St. Joan*.

It was therefore sad news for Liverpool's theatregoers, when on 8th February 1924 it was announced in the local press that the following week's variety bill was to be the last before the building was given over to an army of workmen for demolition, even though this was to be followed by the construction of a magnificent new theatre.

Although the passing of an old theatre was always regarded as a sad occasion, the Empire nevertheless had a starry exit with a variety bill of a reminiscent style, consisting of Coram and Jerry, Marie Dain-

ton, Ernest Hastings, Neil McKay, Tom E. Hughes, the Lombards and Malvine, all well known artistes of the day. There were performances at 6.40pm and 9.00pm until Saturday 16th February 1924 when the old Empire Theatre closed its doors for the last time.

The building was subsequently demolished and construction commenced of the new theatre of the same name which now occupies the site.

1866
STAR MUSIC HALL/STAR THEATRE OF VARIETIES/STAR THEATRE/LIVERPOOL REPERTORY THEATRE/PLAYHOUSE, Williamson Square

---

In the mid nineteenth century a building resembling a dwelling house with entry at the head of stone steps occupied part of the site of the present Playhouse Theatre. The original builders constructed a concert room from the front and back parlours, and with a small stage at one end it was known as the Star Concert Hall in which the proprietor, Jem Ward established harmonic evenings. After Mr. Ward left to take over the York Hotel at the corner of Williamson Square and Tarleton Street, his successor in 1847, a Mr. Hamilton instituted free admission to the concert room, deriving revenue from the sale of first class steaks, chops and wines. The proprietor during the early 1860s, Emmanuel Braham was succeeded in 1866 by David Lazarus, who closed the concert hall on 2nd July for the purpose of demolition and the erection of the New Star Music Hall. To the plans of the distinguished Liverpool architect, Edward Davies, the building was completed in just over five months by the well known building contractors, Messrs. Haigh & Company, at a cost of £22,000. It was described as an excellent structure, and the Victorian facade, an ornament to the square. It remains today, largely unaltered. The excellent stuccoed facade was constructed sevens bays wide and two main storeys with an attic. The first floor was articulated by Corinthian pilasters with a straight entablature above, whilst the attic storey, also with pilasters, had oval windows in the two flanking bays, and circular windows in the centre. Above these at the central highest part of the frontage was a broken triangular pediment, and at this level, at the corners, massive domes were supported by columns.

Internally the building possessed all the attractions that the architect, directors and upholsterers could give. Designed to hold 1,800 to 2,000 people, the hall was semi-circular in shape, with maximum dimensions of 90ft in length, 64ft wide and a height of 60ft. The lower floor was occupied by a few rows of stalls seats in front, the greater part being allocated to small tables and chairs in wood partitioned areas where patrons were served with refreshments by waiters. Extending around the auditorium were two large galleries with tastefully decorated fronts, supported on light iron columns. The seats in these areas were richly upholstered in crimson velvet whilst those of the stalls were covered with red American leather, and all the partitions, tables etc. were of polished mahogany. The stage was stated to be of good size, and the prosce-

nium of elegant design, whilst the drop curtain and beautiful new scenery were the productions of the great scenic artist, William Telbin. The ceiling was adorned by panels for decorative work, and the walls by beautiful ornamental painting and decorating, also splendid mirrors and glasswork. Large refreshment bars provided on the ground and first floors of the auditorium for the sale of wines and spirits etc., and for the illumination of the building, brilliant gas fittings were supplied by Messrs. Defries of London.

The proprietors, Messrs. Ambrose, Isaac Fineberg and David Lazarus, realising the growing important of Liverpool as a great Metropolis of the commercial world, with an increasing demand for musical entertainment, entered upon the under taking with an unusual degree of confidence, in the certain knowledge that the planned high class of entertainment nightly submitted to the public could not fail to meet with the most unprecedented success. But they were also aware that this could only be achieved by the provision of a really first class music hall, which for many years had been a requirement in Liverpool. With this aim in view, the interior was of a similar design to that of the Oxford Theatre in London, and with regard to entertainment this, it was stated was to be most varied with opera, ballet, and a great variety of other performances by an orchestra and chorus of sixty.

The New Star Music Hall was opened on 26th December 1866, when the house was full for the performance which commenced at 7.00pm. The curtain rose to the playing of the National Anthem by the orchestra, and sung by Madame Tonnelier, Prima Donna of Italian opera, and Mr. J. Busfield, the talented English tenor leading the chorus. After an excellent miscellaneous programme of music, Madame Tonnelier and Mrs. D. Saunders distinguished themselves with their singing in a selection from Bellini's opera of *Norma*. There was also a grand ballet entitled *La Fete Des Fleurs* in the performance, which was reported as being of an attractive character with an excellent orchestra led by Herr Bosadneck, with as musical director and pianist Signor G. Operti, formerly pianist to

King Victor Emmanuel of Italy.

The prices of admission were - reserved stalls 1/6d, balconies 1/-, body of the hall 6d and admission to the stalls at 1/- was to gentlemen only by the Houghton Street entrance.

As had been anticipated by the proprietors, the Star was an immediate success for the reason that Isaac Fineberg introduced the best talent, many of the artistes later winning fame and fortune. For many years it was among the leading music halls in the country and an attractive rendezvous for lovers of comedy and music. Those seated on the lower floor at the tables were served with refreshments by waiters as the Chairman, hammer in hand at one side of the stage announced the turns.

After taking over the Theatre Hotel in the square in 1872, David Lazarus severed his connection with the Star, of which the proprietors were then Messrs. Ambrose, Isaac Fineberg and Noah Lees. Later when Ambrose sold his interest, Fineberg and Lees were the proprietors with Harris Fineberg, the son of the former as manager.

Due to advancing years, Isaac Fineberg decided to throw off the responsibilities of the theatre, and in 1895 sold his interest to a company known as the Liverpool Palace of Varieties Ltd. His partnership with Noah Lees ended on 16th May 1896 when it was announced that under the control of the new proprietors, the name of the theatre was to be changed to the Star Theatre of Varieties, and with the esteemed Harris Fineberg continuing in the position of manager, a prosperous future was predicted for the popular place of entertainment.

The theatre was immediately reopened on 18th May 1896 with a first class vaudeville company of 13 'turns' on the programme which was nightly enjoyed by large audiences.

It transpired however that the theatre in its original form was to be open for a short time only, a scheme of extensive alterations at a cost of about £14,000 having been undertaken on acquisition by the new owners who closed the theatre on 8th August 1896. The plans, which included re-construction of the auditorium were drawn up by Harry Percival, architect of The Strand, London and from the capital also came the builders, Messrs. Lilly & Lilly. The old balconies were demolished and replaced by a slightly curved dress circle and a gallery of a similar form above. The former terminated with two boxes at either side of the stage, and directly below these were two further boxes, just above ground floor level, the appearance of these being enhanced by expensive red plush drapes. The auditorium was described as a model of neatness and good taste, the classic carving and cornice work harmonising beautifully with the draperies, seat coverings and carpets. Seating throughout consisted of tip-up chairs, those of the circle in ruby plush, and those of the boxes and stalls in the colour of old gold. Previously lit by gas, an important improvement was the ample provision of electric light by the Phangos Electric Light Company of Liverpool. The main entrance was unchanged, but led into an improved vestibule of attractive appearance, from which corridors led to the stalls, staircases led to the circle and gallery and there was a separate entrance to the pit from Houghton Street.

Retaining the name of Star Theatre of Varieties, the re-opening was initially arranged for Saturday 26th December 1896, but there was a late decision to postpone this until Monday, 28th December. It was announced that after entire structural alterations, this was the most perfectly appointed theatre in the provinces. Harris Fineberg remained in the position of manager, and for the re-opening, a high class vaudeville entertainment was engaged. The doors were opened at 7.00pm for the performance at 7.30pm and representing a considerable increase over those of 1866, the admission prices were - private boxes 10/6d to 21/-, fauteuiles 3/-, orchestra stalls and dress circle 2/-, pit 1/- and gallery 6d.

This proved however to be a short term venture for in the spring of 1898, a dramatic licence was applied for, and having been granted, the last variety entertainment was presented on Saturday 28th May 1898, when the curtain was rung down on the theatre's long history as a music hall.

Liverpool Palace of Varieties Ltd. then relinquished control to the manager, Harris Fineberg, under whose able proprietorship the dramatic season at the Star Theatre was immediately inaugurated on Monday 30th May 1898 by Rollo Balmain's company with the play *Hoodman Blind*, Wilson Barrett's great success direct from the Princess Theatre, London.

Mr. Fineberg's policy of catering for the popular taste with 'blood and thunder' melodrama at popular prices was successful, the theatre prospering for many years until this era came to an end on 10th June 1911 with Morton Powell's drama, *Driving a Girl to Distraction*. The closure coincided with the start of the usual summer vacation at this and three other dramatic houses in the city, but the Star was closed for five months, Harris Fineberg having agreed to sell the theatre to the Liverpool Repertory Company. The sale was agreed one day over lunch at the Adelphi Hotel when Sir Charles Reilly, a professor of architecture at the University of Liverpool, and first chairman of the company, and Clifford Muspratt, a member of a then famous Liverpool family, and one of the first directors, entertained Harris Fineberg and agreed the purchase price of £28,000 of which £22,000 was to remain on mortgage.

The theatre was acquired by the company to provide a permanent home for repertory in Liverpool, the term, repertory being applied to the system by which a series of plays was produced, and as far as possible, acted by the same company. The idea was founded by Miss Annie Elizabeth Fredericka Horniman, who opened the rebuilt Gaiety Theatre, Manchester with her own company in 1908. This having closed for lack of support in 1920 by which time other earlier repertory theatres by different founders were also closed, leaving the by then renamed Liverpool Playhouse as the senior repertory theatre in the country. The reason for this was the greater public demand in Liverpool, from which a group of young enthusiasts journeyed to Manchester to see repertory at the Gaiety, and formed the Liverpool Playgoers Society. Their campaign for a repertory theatre in Liverpool resulted in a six week's experimental season in 1911 at Kelly's Theatre in Paradise Street. The theatre was leased to the

Liverpool Repertory Company, and under the direction of the well known actress of the time, Miss Darragh, who was never billed with her Christian name, and Basil Dean, the company's first producer, the opening production was John Galsworthy's Strife. In later years Basil Dean went on to a long and distinguished career with the London stage as actor and producer, before he became a well known director of British films in the 1930s.

At that time, to many people, repertory was synonymous with everything that was, dramatically speaking, dull, drab and boring. The plays being the most highbrow

of the highbrow. The critics jeered at the company for believing there was sufficient support for a permanent theatre, although they nevertheless proceeded with their plans for the Star Theatre, but for which the success of later years may never have been achieved.

Under the direction of Sir Charles Reilly and Professor Stanley D. Adshead, the first Professor of Town Planning at the Liverpool University and a brilliant architect in his own right, who generously accepted payment in shares, the Star Theatre was redesigned, modernised and redecorated at a cost of about £4,000. The auditorium was then reconstructed in its present style, providing a greatly reduced seating capacity of 760, including six rows of seats on each of the two curved balconies, supported by light iron columns, with fronts decorated by trellis-type plaster work. The balconies curved around to the splayed walls at either side of the tall 30ft wide proscenium where the previous four boxes were replaced by a single pedimented box with Greek revival style pillastered panels above, and the exit way below adorned by elaborately carved plaster mouldings.

The stage was enlarged to a depth of 32ft, this being among the requirements in that part of the building of Basil Dean, supported by George Harris, an artist whose work was to bring distinction to the company's more ambitious productions. But these improvements were only achieved as a result of their efforts to prevent the architect from spending too much on the auditorium and other areas. It is acknowledged however, that Adshead's brilliant reconstruction of the old beer cellar, in which many pints had been served to patrons of the Star, into a charming foyer, where patrons could circulate during intervals, was then and remains an outstanding feature of the theatre, in later years accommodating a licenced bar and coffee lounge.

The first board of directors of the Liverpool Repertory Company consisted of twelve prominent citizens, drawn from various sides of Liverpool life, which Basil Dean called his jury, each member being an authority in his own line, and anxious to give the theatre the benefit of his own special experience. But in view of the fact that none of them possessed technical knowledge or had any experience of theatrical management, the responsibility of the permanent home of Liverpool repertory fell heavily on the shoulders of Basil Dean, whose own knowledge was limited to the short season at Kelly's Theatre. It is recorded that battles royal took place in the Board Room every Thursday, when the directors, each with his own individual ideas on the running of the theatre and the selection of future plays, vetoed rather than selected them. But such an excess of enthusiasm proved in the long term to be good for the theatre and for Mr. Dean who in the years to come was grateful for the vigorous grooming in responsibility which he had received.

Then known as the Liverpool Repertory Theatre in a blaze of glory and general excitement the doors were opened at 7.00pm on 11th November 1911 for the performance at 7.30pm of *The Admirable Crichton* by J.M. Barrie. Civic representation was by the attendance of the Lord Mayor of Liverpool, Lord Derby, who occupied one of the boxes in the crowded auditorium where many well known Liverpool people attended to cordially inaugurate the reign of repertory. The production by Basil Dean was performed by the Repertory company which consisted of James Hearn, Estelle Winwood, Arthur Chesney, Aida Jenoure, Ronald Squire, Hazel Thompson and others. At this time the prices of admission were - private boxes £2/2/-, stalls 4/-, dress circle 3/- and gallery 1/-.

For about two years the theatre was well attended with plays which reflected the change in the social pattern, such as John Glasworthy's *Justice* and Ibsen's *Pillars of Society*. But after that period, audiences dwindled and before recovery could be made

STAR NEW GRAND MUSIC HALL, WILLIAMSON-SQUARE, LIVERPOOL.

PROPRIETORS: MESSRS. AMBROSE FINEBERG & DAVID.

THE ABOVE MAGNIFICENT HALL WILL OPEN THIS DAY (WEDNESDAY), THE 26TH INSTANT.

The PROPRIETORS, in referring to the growing importance of this great Metropolis of the Commercial World, and the increasing demand for

MUSICAL ENTERTAINMENTS,

Have entered upon this stupendous undertaking with an unusual degree of confidence, feeling sure that the HIGH CLASS OF ENTERTAINMENT they will nightly have the honour of submitting to the public cannot fail to meet with the most unprecedented success. It is, perhaps, hardly necessary for them to observe that a really first-class Music Hall in Liverpool has been a great requisition for many years past; and they felt it would be well as to attempt anything of the kind unless it could be carried out on the London principle in every sense of the word, viz., with regard to the ... WITH ... OF THE BUILDING, CLASS OF ENTERTAINMENT, & MANAGEMENT. In all the important Items they have been singularly fortunate. The site is in the heart of Liverpool. That distinguished architect Mr. Edward Davies, of Liverpool, has erected a building that may safely be pronounced second to none throughout the United Kingdom. They have secured the services of some of the GREATEST ARTISTES, in all the leading branches of the profession; and the management of each department has been entrusted to gentlemen of well known experience and reputation, who will assist the Proprietors in carrying out the various arrangements in a style worthy this GREAT ESTABLISHMENT.

came the outbreak of World War I in August 1914. Basil Dean resigned to join the armed forces as did several male members of the company, and Madge McIntosh was appointed as producer. The directors then found themselves with an expensive company under contract, and a programme of plays arranged with which, in the circumstances of war time there was the prospect of three months poor business, resulting in a probable weekly loss of up to £200. Added to the acute state of the theatre's finances, this forced the directors to consider closing the theatre. This would probably have been the case had it not been for Estelle Winwood one of the original members, who produced a scheme for continuing the Autumn season by the formation of an Artists' and Staffs' Commonwealth. Madge McIntosh as producer was at the head of this with manager Thomas J.Piggott. Artistes, Musicians, stage staff and all employed agreed to run the theatre for a fixed minimum living wage, reserving the right to close down should the receipts fail to provide for this. The directors received a limited share in receipts to an amount sufficient to cover standing charges. The Commonwealth Scheme was operational from 19th September 1914 and the Liverpool theatregoers gave it their whole hearted support for the high standard of plays which included, *The Doctor's Dilemma*, *The Fugitive*, *Trelawney of the Wells* and *Twelfth Night*. In this way, the theatre was run on a shoestring until the end of the war in 1918 when paid contracts were resumed.

At this time the theatre was known as The Playhouse, the change of name having been made from 19th February 1917, coinciding with the presentation of J.M. Barrie's *What Every Woman Knows*.

There were several changes of producer during the ensuing five years, but it is acknowledged that the most successful was William Armstrong, formerly a member of the acting company, whose regime between 1922 and 1944 represented a prosperity and continuity of policy as a result of his flair for selecting plays,which he knew the public wished to see. He also had an uncanny genius for finding young talented artists to join the resident company. The Playhouse therefore produced stars whose names became well known world-wide, among the many now best remembered being, Rex Harrison, Robert Donat, Michael Redgrave and Diana Wynyard, all of whom were stars of British films during the 1930's.

With justification it has been stated that the Liverpool Playhouse has enriched the stage to quite an extraordinary extent, and that probably more of our best actors and actresses have learned their art in Williamson Square than in any other part of the country, many of them never looking back after departing to other locations.

In addition to his continual attention to plays and casting, William Armstrong introduced a new type of play-bill to advertise them, changing from the old heavy type, which conveyed an impression of old fashioned vigour, to a new style, chaste, elegant and discreetly middle class. This was more appropriate to the new theatre public, many seekers of melodrama having been drawn to the cinemas.

The year after William Armstrong was appointed as producer, a lady who was to be among the theatre's longest serving and most successful managers, Maud Carpenter took over the position of business manager and licencee following the retirement of the General Manager, A.S. Pigott in March 1923. Maud Carpenter had joined the company as a junior box office clerk at Kelly's Theatre, but having been trained as a secretary, she became assistant manager to Mr. Pigott for five years until her final appointment. It was then the subject of much criticism, a woman having been chosen. But her critics were soon proved wrong, for whilst ladies had previously been successful in the position at other theatres, Maud Carpenter was outstanding in that she chose to devote her life to the management of the Playhouse.

The success of the repertory company was interrupted during World War II in 1941 with the heavy bombing of Merseyside, and although escaping damage despite the surrounding devastation, the directors considered it wise to close for the reasons that artists were not easy to find, many men and women were serving in the forces, or engaged on work of national importance, and there were transport difficulties under black-out conditions. But nevertheless, the Playhouse was soon reopened, having been leased in 1942 to the Old Vic Company, who had been bombed out of their London Theatre in the Waterloo Road. They introduced many distinguished artists and several talented producers, presenting mainly classical plays, differing considerable from those to which Playhouse audiences had become accustomed. The company nevertheless enjoyed considerable success despite war time conditions, by attracting different audiences, mainly of young people in uniform, some seeing 'live' plays for the first time, many regulars having left Liverpool for various reasons. In the position of a kind

of liaison officer, Maud Carpenter remained as manager and licencee, and the Old Vic Company occupied the theatre until the autumn of 1946 when the directors resumed control. John Fernald was appointed as producer and a resident company was engaged, the new producer had two practical ambitions, the first of which was never achieved, to make the Playhouse the National Theatre of the North, where could be seen the best representative drama of the western world. The second was to create a company of actors, which through unity of aim and understand-

ing of each others methods, would be capable of rising to any opportunity which might arise. The year 1948 saw a company

which, after considerable trial and error, had become something of which any director could be proud. The production of *The Cherry Orchard* by Anton Chekhov, the Russian dramatist, went from the Playhouse to the St. James's theatre in London, in June of that years, and remains the Liverpool company's finest hour, their fame, drawing a visit from Queen Mary at the last performance became part of theatrical history.

After his departure to the Arts Theatre, London in 1949, John Fernald was succeeded by Gerald Cross, who had been an active member of the company for several seasons. Choosing a young and enthusiastic company of artists, some with considerable experience, and others on the threshold of their careers, during his two years' regime, he was responsible for at least four new plays, and at the director's request took over the title role in Shakespeare's *King Richard II*.

William Stoker, who was appointed as producer in 1951 was interested in the American stage plays and introduced them to Playhouse audiences for the first time in the country. But his regime experienced difficult times from about the mid-fifties due to the impact of television, and attendances as at most theatres and cinemas decreased. But at the time of opening the 1959 season Mr. Stoker was in a position to state his feeling that the theatre had weathered the television storm, due to slightly increased attendances. Opening with J.B. Priestley's *Dangerous Corner* the season included a wide range of plays, but excluding avant garde productions, which were considered to be a financial risk. Although internally during the summer closure, work had been limited to maintenance, outside the theatre a big change was observed, the pale blue painted facade giving to Williamson Square, according to reports an almost Mediterranean appearance and after dark, the frontage was floodlit, whilst the domes were illuminated from within.

Two years later, in November 1961, the Golden Jubilee of the Playhouse was celebrated with a Gala Performance of Sheridan's *School for Scandal*, attended by Princess Marina. There was a 60lb birthday cake replica of the theatre, and for the sum of five shillings, patrons could purchase an excellent brochure, which included a letter of congratulations from the Lord Mayor of Liverpool, Peter McKernan, and numerous autobiographies including those of Basil Dean and Maud Carpenter, a director of the theatre since 1945, whose devotion to it could never be repaid.

The end of an era came on Saturday 8th June 1962 when Maud Carpenter retired after over 50 years with the theatre. It was a night of tears and cheers, bouquets and applause after the final curtain of the play *Reflections In The Square*, when Maud Carpenter went on stage to a tremendous ovation, her speech stressing the value of

team work, which had been responsible for the success and long survival of the Playhouse.

This was the beginning of a period of great change. Willard Stoker departed to London for the production of plays in the West End. For the opening of the new season in August 1962, it was announced that the new team of C.D. Hamilton-Moore as General Manager and Bernard Hepton formerly at the Birmingham Repertory as producer, would bring new ideas. The season commenced on 14th August with Peter Ustinov's comedy, *Romanoff and Juliet* performed by a cast almost new to the Playhouse.

The 1960s was an era of significant improvements, commencing with the demolition of the adjoining cafe at the left-hand side of the frontage, and replaced by a single storey extension, painted blue to match the main facade, to provide better accommodation for the painting of scenery. In March 1961 a stage lighting control system was installed at the rear of the auditorium at a cost of £8,000, the first of its kind in the country with 750 graduations of light in colour and intensity. A further technical improvement came in January 1964, when new sound amplification equipment was installed for the first new production of the year, *Dr. Angelus* for which was provided more flexible use of sound and music.

But despite the technical improvements, the first half of the 1960s was a period of falling attendances resulting in financial losses. Whether or not connected therewith, June 1965 saw the resignation of C.D. Hamilton-Moore as manager and licensee, and the appointment of his successor, Kay Gardner of the Theatre Royal, Lincoln.

In December 1965 redevelopment plans by architect Colin Wilson at a cost of £220,000 were announced, and in April 1966 the theatre was closed for work to begin on the first phase. The stage was enlarged, and eleven new dressing rooms with splendid mirrors and lighting were provided, also a larger Green Room, rehearsal rooms and a workshop. A new oil fired central heating system was installed and externally the old lead lined domes,

which weighed over a ton were replaced by new domes of glass fibre, 400lbs in weight.

The second phase of the alterations for which the theatre was closed in the summer of 1967 involved the construction of the now long familiar glass tower and new main entrance at the left-hand side of the old facade, bridging the hundred years' gap between this and the new Ravenscroft precinct. The architect had faced the problem of how to design the extension so that it would be dominant, and yet not detract from the charm of the old facade, and also to be taken into account was that the Victorians built in such vastly different styles and the fact that the extension had to be of considerable height in order to link the public space with the old auditorium at every level from basement to gallery.

Below the tower, the new, wide main entrance with two lines of metal framed doors led into the spacious foyer with circular booking office in the centre, cloakroom immediately on the left, access to the stalls left and right, and an open staircase to the first floor. There in addition to the circle entrances, audience facilities were extended with a full restaurant, named the Redgrave Room, after the famous actor, Sir Michael Redgrave, also a buffet bar, whilst in the evenings, the Star Buttery was open for pre and post theatre meals and interval drinks. Technically, the tower consisted of two main vertical columns of reinforced concrete, the tallest being 55ft. All the ribs were left undecorated providing a spoke-like appearance, and each of the restaurants was linked to the old auditorium by a series of bridges.

Always a point of admiration from visiting actors and guests, the auditorium was enhanced by re-painting in a deep purple colour with the Regency styled designs picked out in white and gold.

On the evening of 12th December 1968 new brilliance was added to the square when the Playhouse celebrated the opening of the new extension, and the new season, with the first of three Gala nights, thereby achieving a great sense of occasion. The play was entitled *The Lyon's Mail* but the real star of the evening was the building, for which a specially extended interval gave the

audience a chance to explore the new foyers and bars etc., and to discover how well the old and the new had been blended. After touring the extension, Sir Michael Redgrave opened the coffee lounge, of which, later there was also an official opening on 28th October 1968 by the Duchess of Kent, who unveiled a plaque in the foyer.

With a membership of nearly 1,300, and the sale of season tickets considerably ahead of the previous year, a bright future was predicted, also favourable was the fact that despite earlier season's losses, the capital debit of building the extension had been wiped out. An added attraction to follow was the conversion of the former rehearsal room of the third floor into the 100 seat Playhouse Studio, which opened on 20th October 1969 with *Look Back in Anger* by John Osborne.

This coincided with the departure of Kay Gardner, and the appointment of her successor as General Manager and Licensee, Christopher Bullock, whose inestimable services to the theatre during the ensuing six years resulted in his well deserved appointment to the position of Administrative Director in September 1975. At this time, Henry Cotton, Chairman of the board of directors announced the appointment as artistic director of Leslie Lawton, after two and a half years in a similar position at the Palace, Westcliffe-on-Sea. The combination of their individual theatrical skills made these gentlemen a formidable partnership, dedicated to bringing to the Playhouse the very best entertainment of its type on Merseyside. In the early 1980s, at the time of the 70th anniversary of the repertory theatre, Chris Bond and playwright, Bill Morrison, were the new artistic team, and the former having been in charge of the less sophisticated Everyman Theatre, some change of policy was apparent by the choice of Chris Bond's own version of *Dracula,* described as a spine chilling comedy as the main house Christmas attraction for 1981. This was followed on 28th January 1982 by a world premier of *Scrap!* by Bill Morrison and later Alan Bleasdale's *Having a Ball.*

The Playhouse survived through further difficult times in the early 1980s, and certain closure in 1983 was only avoided by

a record breaking 11 weeks run of the smash hit musical *Blood Brothers* by Willy Russell during the period up to 19th March 1983, when it was attended by 55,000 people. Two years later, in the new regime of David Fischel as administrative director and Ian Kellner as artistic director, the 75th anniversary was celebrated with a star studded Gala Night, and a new look restaurant, refurbished and on more open plan lines, with new designs of a more theatrical style. The Playhouse was then again under threat of closure, in this case on health and safety grounds, there being no available funds for urgent internal repairs. The theatre was saved by the Government Business Incentive scheme, from which the Playhouse received £7,500 of the £3m government money allocated for the arts.

In June 1990 the Playhouse was the latest building in the city to rediscover its architectural heritage with a facelift to restore its former Edwardian glory. Liverpool architects, Brock Carmichael Associates were in charge of the work of removing all the seats and the erection of scaffolding for repainting as at present, to emphasise the ornate plaster mouldings, and the laying of a new, specially designed woven carpet.

The work was completed in time for the opening of the new season on 9th July 1990 with a return of Alan Bleasdale's comedy, *Having a Ball*.

In March 1991, the theatre was again in serious financial difficulties, and a campaign to save it headed by Lady Olivier received overwhelming public support. This resulted in the first £50,000 instalment of a £250,000 five years' rescue package, which was handed over by the then Environment Secretary, Michael Heseltine, who helped launch a £1.5m private sector appeal.

Since that time the theatre has also had the benefit of private backing by Liverpool born, West End producer, Bill Kenwright, who has introduced pre London runs of commercial shows. This arrangement having been intended for a period of five years only, the Playhouse has now retuned to its origin as a repertory theatre under the control of artistic director, Richard Williams, who on 11th September 1996 opened his first season with the comedy

Noises Off by Michael Frayn.

At this time, nearing the end of a decade, the Playhouse remains as Merseyside's sole surviving theatre of the victorian era.

> ### 1867
> ### THE PRINCE PATRICK HALL/
> ### THE WELLINGTON HALL/
> ### THE GAIETY THEATRE,
> ### Camden Street

Opposite the site of the recently demolished Trocadero/Gaumont cinema, this hall was constructed from a couple of large dwelling houses by Dr F.C.S. Corry, M.D., who had previously provided entertainment by dioramas at a concert hall in Lord Nelson Street. These having proved to be successful, Dr. Corry decided on a permanent home for the exhibitions, which he named the Prince Patrick Hall, opening on 16th February 1867 with a diorama entitled *Ireland - It's Scenery, Music and Antiquities,* and a company of Hibernian minstrels.

The hall with one of the entrances in Back Commutation Row, then accommodated about 1,500 people, was renamed the Wellington Hall when it was opened with a concert party on 31st December 1868. The following year they were succeeded by Messrs. Craddock and Day, late of the Royal Alexandra and Prince of Wales theatres.. Their stay was also brief since on 1st November 1869, Mr. Alfred Roe, formerly director of the Leeds Theatre of Varieties took over and opened with a change of name to the Wellington Varieties.

Towards the end of 1870, when Mr. Frank Clive was the managing director, the hall became the Gaiety Theatre, and the following year it reverted to the Wellington Hall, but from October 1872 under the direction of a Professor Anderson, it was given the unusual title, The Royal Temple of Magic.

The reopening as the Gaiety Theatre took place on 13th April 1874, when the proprietor, Mr. Naylor Roberts appointed as manager, Mr. (later Sir) Charles Wyndham, who was later to become a famous actor,

performed on the opening night in the play *Committed for Trial*. The theatre, which consisted of stalls, dress circle, pit and gallery had been redecorated for the opening. Charles Wyndham was in the position of manager for only a few weeks, then realising his aim to move to London, where he founded Wyndham's Theatre. Following another short period of ownership by a limited company, the Gaiety was reopened by Mr. C.H Duval on 22nd September 1874 with a comic opera company in La Fille de Madame Angot.

About three years later, Mr. Duval left to take up the management of the Colosseum, Paradise Street and was succeeded by Mr. Harry de Frece, under whose control in the early 1880s, the hall was known as the Gaiety Temperence Theatre. This survived into the 1890s, but after his departure it changed hands several times. Following a period during which the Gaiety was closed, an attempt to reopen it was by made a Mr. Henry Newbold of the city, who applied to the magistrates for a licence. This was however, refused, and the building remained unused until it was eventually converted for commercial requirements in the early years of this century.

> ### 1869
> ### ROTUNDA MUSIC HALL/
> ### ROTUNDA THEATRE,
> ### Stanley Road

The site at the junction of Stanley Road and Kirkdale Road was first occupied in 1863 by a public house, where what were described as 'free and easy' entertainments were presented nightly by vocalists appearing on a small stage. About 1866, the proprietor, Mr. Dennis Grannell introduced plans for the re-siting of the entertainment on a more extensive upper floor where a larger stage was constructed at the Scotland Road end of the building. The largely musical fare was then supplemented by sketches, and at the new entrance in Scotland Road the prices of admission were - boxes, 1/6d, stalls 1/-, and pit 6d.

ROTUNDA MUSIC-HALL, Scotland Road.
Proprietor .... MR. D. GRINNELL.
NEW COMPANY. CROWDED HOUSES.
The following first class Artistes appear every Evening:—Mr. and Mrs.
SWEENY. Comic Duettists.—Mrs. F. R. PHILLIPS, Serio Comic.—
Miss KATE BELFORD, Serio Comic.—Miss F. MACDONALD, Serio
Comic and Danseuse.—Miss ROSE CLARENDON, Ballad Vocalist.—
BROTHERS FRITZ, four in number, Gymnasts, &c.—G. BUCK-
STONE, the great London Comic.—A. A. COX, Star American Come-
dian, Vocalist, &c.—SAM PRIDE, Banjo Soloist.—J. FERANDO, Jig
Dancer.
Doors open at Half-past Six. Concert to commence at Seven precisely.
Admission: Boxes 1s 6d; Stalls 1s; Body, 6d, by the new Entrance
in Scotland-road; Gallery, 3d; Reserved Seats, 6d. entrance Stanley
road.

After further reconstruction with the addition of a gallery, the establishment was reopened as the Rotunda Music Hall by Dennis Grannell on 23rd November 1869, when a Grand Concert was given under the distinguished patronage of His Worship the Mayor, J. Hubback, Esq. Two days later on 25th November, a performance by specially engaged first class artists commenced precisely at 7.00pm. On that evening it was reported the exterior of the building was brilliantly illuminated by Mr. G. Anley, firework artist, and there was also a grand magnesium balloon ascent, prior to the opening by Mr. Anley. Prices of admission were similar to those previously charged but with the addition of gallery seats at 3d, and reserved seats at 6d at the entrance in Stanley Road. The proceeds from the performance were in aid of the nearby Stanley Hospital.

Mr. Charles Wood, for five years musical director at the Adelphi Theatre, Christian Street came to the Rotunda on 1st August 1870 to take up the position of musical and stage director, and was associated with the theatre for over 25 years. For the Christmas of 1870 the attraction was the pantomime *Dick Whittington*, and following its run, concert and vaudeville companies were interspersed with dramatic plays from April 1874 when the first stock

company was inaugurated. This became the regular form of entertainment due to increased public demand and to provide for this, a new gallery, balcony, stage and sixteen private boxes were constructed, during which the theatre remained open by the use of tarpaulins as a roof covering.

With the exception of concerts from 17th August 1874 and the Christmas pantomime, *Puss In Boots*, which ran from 26th December for four weeks, plays by the stock company were continued for four seasons. During this time, in 1875, Mr. James Kiernan, who was destined to become a leading figure in the sphere of 'live' entertainment in Liverpool, commenced as a checktaker at the Rotunda for a salary of nine shillings per week, and after subsequent promotions was appointed to the position of assistant to Charles Wood.

Plays by the stock company at the old Rotunda came to an end on Saturday 7th July 1877 with *The Shaughraun*, the theatre being destroyed by fire early on the following Monday. The proprietor Dennis Grannell was immediately desirous of building a new and larger theatre, but he was aware that due to the destruction of the old theatre by fire, means of ingress and egress in any future plans would be of the utmost importance to the city magistrates in their consideration to the granting of a new licence. In order to obtain the best arrangements in this respect, Mr. Grannell consulted an eminent architect, Mr. C.J. Phipps, F.S.A. of London, who had been the architect of about twenty theatres throughout the country. From his plans, the building contractors, Messrs. Haigh and Company of Liverpool constructed a most imposing five storey building with principal elevations to Stanley Road and Kirkdale Road connected by a curved corner, surmounted by a dome at the end nearest Scotland Road.

The frontages were of light and dark brick, and a huge canopy extended along that adjacent to Stanley Road. Internally, above the basement area in which were two bowling alleys and a carpenter's workshop, the ground floor was allocated for a foyer connecting the Stanley Road and Kirkdale Road entrances, also a billiard room and a public house at the Scotland Road end.

From the foyer, staircases led up to the stalls at first floor level, and from the landings continued up to the dress circle, amphicircle and the gallery. The auditorium was about 60ft in length and greatest width with the orchestra pit in front of the 40ft deep stage. On the stalls floor this was flanked on either side by a box, whilst

NEW ROTUNDA THEATRE.
Proprietor..................Mr. D. Grannell.
GRAND OPENING NIGHT
TO-NIGHT (FRIDAY), DECEMBER 20,
UNDER THE PATRONAGE OF
HIS WORSHIP THE MAYOR.
THE RENOWNED
CARL ROSA OPERA COMPANY,
COMPRISING THE FOLLOWING DISTINGUISHED ARTISTES:—
MADAME VANZINI,   MISS GEORGINA BURNS,
MISS JOSEPHINE YORKE,
MISS ELLA COLLINS,   MISS JULIA GAYLORD,
MR. JOSEPH MAAS,   MR. CHARLES LYALL,
MR. L. CADWALADER,
MR. FRED C. PACKARD,
MR. F. H. CELLI,   MR. SNAZELLE,
MR. LESLIE CROTTY,   MR. DENBIGH NEWTON,
MR. HERBERT LAWRENCE,
MR. MULLER.   MR. HENRY POPE,
FULL BAND, CHORUS, AND BALLET.
CONDUCTOR..................MR. CARL ROSA
Stage Manager..................Mr. G. H. Betjemann.
Musical Prompter..................Mr. W. J. Petre.
Chorus Master..................Mr. John Pew.
Acting Manager and Treasurer..Mr. J. D. M'Laren.
THE NATIONAL ANTHEM WILL BE SUNG BY THE
ENTIRE COMPANY,
WITH FULL ORCHESTRAL ACCOMPANIMENT.
AFTER WHICH
Sir Julius Benedict's Grand Romantic Opera,
THE LILY OF KILLARNEY.
Hardress Cregan..................Mr. Fred C. Packard
Myles na Coppaleen..............Mr. Charles Lyall
Mr. Corrigan..................Mr. Leahy
Father Tom..................Mr. Snazelle
Danny Mann..................Mr. Leslie Crotty
Mr. O'Moore..................Mr. Dwyer
Hyland Creagh..................Mr. Muller
Miss Anne Chute..................Miss Georgina Burns
Mrs. Cregan..................Miss Josephine Yorke
Sheelah..................Miss Ella Collins
AND
Eily O'Connor..................Miss Julia Gaylord
IN THE LAST ACT AN IRISH JIG WILL BE DANCED
BY
MISS JOSEPHINE & MISS ANNE WARREN.
Doors open at Seven. National Anthem at 7.50.
Opera at Night. Carriages at 10.30.
On SATURDAY, the 21st instant, Balfe's
BOHEMIAN GIRL.
Thaddeus..................Mr. Joseph Maas
Count Arnheim..................Mr. F. H. Celli
Florestine..................Mr. Charles Lyall
Devilshoof..................Mr. Snazelle
Queen of the Gipsies..........Miss Josephine Yorke
Buda..................Miss Burgess
AND
Arline..................Madame Vanzini
Doors open at Seven. National Anthem at 7.50.
Opera at Eight. Carriages at Ten.
Prices of admission for the above Two Nights—Private Boxes, from Two to Five Guineas; Dress Circle and Orchestra Stalls, 4s.; Pit Stalls, 1s.; Pit and Amphi-Circle, 2s.; Gallery, 1s.
Box plan may be seen and seats secured, at the Theatre, open Twelve to Two daily.
Entrance to Boxes, Dress Circle, and Orchestra Stalls, Stanley-road. Entrance to Pit, Gallery, Pit Stalls, and Amphi-Circle, Scotland-road.
On MONDAY, the 23rd instant,
Dion Boucicault's Great Irish Drama,
THE SHAUGHRAUN.
MR. CHARLES SULLIVAN and Company of Specially
Selected Artistes.
For full particulars, prices of admission, &c., see future
advertisements.

above, the front of the dress circle curved around the sides terminating with three boxes, a line of these also being constructed at the rear. The amphicircle, also with a curved front, terminated with a box at either side of the stage, and high above, the gallery front curved to the side walls. The stalls floor accommodated about 700 persons. The first tier comprising the dress circle and boxes, about 740, and the upper circle and gallery about 350, made a total capacity of 1,790. There was also ample standing room in the various parts for about 400 persons, and for those patrons desirous of a drink before the performance or during the interval, a licensed bar was provided at the rear on all floors with the exception of the gallery.

A special session of the borough magistrates was held at the police court in Dale Street on 12th December 1878 to consider an application by Dennis Grannell for the performance of stage plays at the new Rotunda Theatre. In view of the anticipated enquiry with regard to public safety in case of fire or panic, the session was attended by the architect, Mr. Phipps, who came specially from London to ensure the magistrates regarding the most satisfactory arrangements. He stated that the separation of the various departments by thick brick walls and the auditorium from the stage by a fire proof safety curtain would ensure that any fire would be confined to the place of its source. In addition a greater than usual number of exits had been provided so that in an emergency, the theatre could be emptied in four minutes.

The licence was unanimously granted and the grand opening of the new Rotunda Theatre took place on Friday, 20th December 1878 under the patronage of His Worship the Mayor of Bootle, Edward Grindley. The doors were opened at 7.00pm for the performance at 8.00pm of Sir Julius Benedict's Grand Romantic Opera *The Lily of Killarney* by the Carl Rosa Opera Company of distinguished artistes, and full orchestra conducted by Mr. Carl Rosa. On Saturday, 21st instant there was a change to Balfe's opera *The Bohemian Girl* and prices of admission were - private boxes from two to five guineas, dress circle and orchestra stalls 6/-, pit stalls 4/-, pit and amphicircle 2/- and gallery 1/-. Entrances to the boxes, dress circle and orchestra stalls were in Stanley Road, whilst patrons of the lower priced parts of the house used the Kirkdale Road entrance.

On the following Monday, plays

In March 1888 the theatre became one of the limited liability companies under the title Rotunda Theatre Company Ltd., of which the directorate included the Mayor of Bootle, then John Howard, Captain, R.B. Bainbridge, former manager, Charles Wood as secretary, and Dennis Grannell, the for-

The next change of ownership was in 1898, when the theatre was acquired by Messrs. Bent's Brewery Co. Ltd., and Charles Wood, then manager was succeeded by Matthew Montgomery. The interior was re-constructed in 1899 and although no details of this appear to have been recorded,

which had been the principal attraction at the old theatre, returned with Irish dramas presented by Charles Sullivan and Company, later followed by plays again by the stock company, the first in the new theatre, where the first pantomime, *Dick Whittington* commenced on 26th December 1879.

mer proprietor, who sold the property to the company for the sum of £25,000 of which £5,000 in £1 shares was allotted to Mr. Grannell in part payment of the purchase price, for which he transferred the theatre, the billiard room and the American-style bowling alleys to the new syndicate.

it was reported that so great was the transformation that returning patrons gazed around in sheer wonderment. The re-opening on 4th September 1899 was with the play, *The Fenian*, performed by Hubert O'Grady and Company.

In 1903 Matthew Montgomery retired from the management and was succeeded by his son, Matthew, who continued to advance the reputation of the Rotunda as one of the leading centres of melodrama in the provinces, originally built up by Charles Wood. This type of entertainment attracted large numbers of sailors due to the closeness of the theatre to the north Liverpool docks, as had been the case at the old Drury Lane, when the Pier Head and the old dock were the only mooring places for ships. The policy of plays and a pantomime at Christmas was continued until 1917 during which time the repertoire was not entirely devoted to melodrama, since it included - *Hamlet*, *Jim the Penman*, *Mary, Queen of Scots* and *East Lynne* etc. Stage plays with motion pictures on the bioscope as an added attraction were presented between 1912 and 1917, when following the end of a special return visit of the pantomime *Robinson Crusoe* on 24th February, the change was made to revues and variety performances.

The latest novelty, an all black revue, *Coloured Society* was presented during the week commencing 5th March 1917 at 6.50pm and 9pm, supported by pictures on the Bioscope. This was followed by a comedy revue, *The Dream Girl*, after which the first variety bill commenced on 19th March. But more noteable was that of the following week, for it was headed by the well known comedian Robb Wilton, whose Liverpool debut had been at the Theatre Royal, Anfield in 1890. This brought forth the comment in the local press that the Rotunda had made a capital entry into the new form of entertainment. This continued throughout the 1920s and 1930s, and until week ending 21st September 1940, during which the theatre was completely destroyed by enemy action. The last performances were of Star Variety with a bill of first class acts once nightly at 7pm.

The site was cleared some time after the war and was subsequently laid out with grass and small trees as it remains to date.

1875 THE SEFTON THEATRE, Park Road

This rectangular hall, originally used for various kinds of entertainment was converted in 1875 into a theatre for the presentation of dramatic plays, the south end of Liverpool having been without a playhouse since the closure of the Royal Park Theatre in Parliament Street. The Sefton, which had 800 seats in the stalls and 300 in the balcony was opened by Mr C.H. Duval, formerly a well known entertainer at the Queen's Theatre in Paradise Street, and at that time also in control of the Gaiety Theatre, Camden Street.

Mr Duval's reputation having preceded him, there was a full house for the opening of the Sefton Theatre on 21st September 1875 with the comedy *A Bird in the Hand is Worth Two in the Bush*.

A few years later Mr Duval was succeeded as lessee by a Mr R. Mulvey, who renamed the house the Royal Sefton Theatre, presenting drama by his stock company, interspersed with variety performances.

In 1895 the Sefton became the latest addition to the music halls operated by James Kiernan, who had achieved great and well deserved success with this type of entertainment at the Westminster Music Hall, Kirkdale, the Paddington Palace and the Park Palace, Mill Street. When in the early years of the present century there was some decline in the popularity of the music Hall, the Sefton was among the first closures, then being converted into a billiard hall which was open until 1911.

In 1912 the hall was converted into the Park Royal Picture House. It was opened by a Mr George F. Dixon, and from 1919 continued as a cinema by a small company, Park Theatres Ltd. The closure was in May 1924 when an application for the renewal of the licence was refused.

1882 THE HAYMARKET MUSIC HALL, Beau Street

This large music hall with seating for over 2,500 people was situated off Cazneau Street beyond its junction with Scotland Road in an area severely affected by bombing during World War II, which included the destruction of the large Cazneau Street Market. The location of the Haymarket would now be even more difficult to establish since, apart from war damage, the entire area including Cazneau Street was redeveloped during the 1970s with the construction of the approach area to the Wallasey tunnel.

The Haymarket Music Hall was opened on Monday 27th November 1882 by Mr William Kerr with Mr W. Thomas as manager and scenic artist. It was designed for the purpose of presenting two separate performances nightly, a special feature of the auditorium being the provision of ample exits at the front of the hall on both floors, the balcony having an extension along either side. Crushing and inconvenience by delay in entry and exit were thereby avoided, patrons of the first performance leaving at the rear of the building as those for the second performance entered at the front.

After Mr Kerr severed his connection with the hall, he was succeeded by Messrs. Alfred Farrell and Frederick Willmot, the latter named later being in sole control, at which time the admission prices ranged from one penny to a shilling.

The entertainment included sketches by the jovial Joe Elvin, and the Star Comiques of London who visited the hall in turns. It was also one of the many places in Liverpool where aspiring talent could obtain an appearance in the style of the Carroll Levis Discoveries during the 1930s.

The last information concerning the Haymarket indicates that it was successfully managed by Mr Willmot until 1906 when Edwin W. Smith, formerly of the Parthenon Music Hall became the lessee and manager.

1887
THE WESTMINSTER MUSIC HALL/DORIC TALKIE THEATRE,
Smith Street, Kirkdale

The location of this small but popular north end music hall was between Kirkdale Road and Westminster Road. Previously used as a club, it was converted into a theatre and opened by Thomas Montgomery and James Kiernan on 11th April 1887 with J.H. Milburn and a good variety company.

During the following year the auditorium was altered and enlarged to accommodate an audience of 650 including a balcony with straight extensions to the front at either side of the proscenium.

After about two years James Kiernan left to concentrate his attention upon his new acquisition, the Paddington Palace, Matthew Montgomery took over control and was succeeded by his son, also Matthew, when the former left in 1898 to take up the position of manager at the Rotunda Theatre.

Music hall and variety entertainment continued until 1908 when this was one of the music halls acquired by the Weisker Brothers for the showing of motion pictures. The company they formed for this was Weisker's Picture Palaces Ltd. Later known as the Westminster Hall Cinema it was taken over in 1921 by the W. Gordon's Circuit which also operated several cinemas in Liverpool suburbs.

There was another change of proprietor in 1932 when the Westminster was purchased by H.E. Radam, proprietor of the Roscommon, also a former music hall. With a change of name to the Doric Talkie Theatre, the Grand Opening was on 4th April 1932 when the feature film was entitled *The Criminal Code* featuring Walter Huston. The matinee commenced at 3pm and the evening performances were at 6.40 and 8.45pm. Admission prices were low even considering the year, being only 4d in the stalls, 6d and 9d in the balcony, whilst matinee prices were reduced to 3d and 4d. The sound equipment by RCA Phototone was stated to be the best procurable, and the most perfect in the district.

The Doric had been a cinema for about nine years when in 1941 it was among the entertainment houses destroyed during an air raid.

1888
THE SHAKESPEARE THEATRE,
Fraser Street

The announcement in June 1888 that the new Shakespeare Theatre was to open in the following August aroused an amount of interest in the new venture, but as Liverpool theatregoers already had three first class houses on which to bestow their patronage, speculation was rife as to the ultimate success or failure of the rival establishments.

At that time, drama in Liverpool had considerably degenerated during the previous few years, and whilst authorities were divided on the reason for this, it was generally admitted that really first class productions were usually well attended. The question was, whether there were a sufficient number of good productions to supply a multiplication of theatres in the town with profitable business.

Recollections of times past in Liverpool, and an ambition to see the town in the full enjoyment of a new lease of legitimate theatrical life, mainly induced Mr. Ellis Brammall, Jnr., an extensive and practical builder, to institute the erection of the splendid building in Fraser Street. Hence Liverpool could claim the distinguished honour of having, with the exception of the Memorial Theatre at Stratford-on-Avon, the only Shakespeare Theatre in England, a building from floor to roof worthy of its great name.

For eighteen months a large number of workmen under the personal supervision of Ellis Brammall, were employed in the construction of the theatre, of which a description is as follows:-

The substantial building had a wide, imposing, three storey frontage, adorned by pilasters with carved capitals of the central section, and a great amount of carved stonework formed an attractive setting for the lines of windows at first and second floor levels. Other features were the words - Comedy - Tragedy - Music carved in stone and the bust of Shakespeare below the theatre name. At ground level were sited six arched entrances, each with a pair of glass-panelled doors, the three largest in the centre formed the main entrance, and all were surmounted by a massive iron and glass canopy, upon which the principal lighting by electricity, at either end was from two large, lantern-style clear-glass shaded fittings. The main entrance led into the magnificent foyer with carved mahogany booking office, direct access to the stalls, and an attractive marble staircase to the first floor lounge and dress circle. The rich carpets, the beautifully designed stained-glass windows with sumptuous curtains, the richly bevelled mirrors, and the whole surmounted by a tastefully panelled ceiling were all items of general admiration. On the first floor, particular attention was devoted to the dress circle lounge. Considered to rival that of any theatre in England, it was luxuriously furnished with comfortable settees. There was a superb ceiling and the wall fittings of polished oak were exquisitely carved with representations from Shakespeare. A remarkable feature on every tier was that the crush rooms abutting the seating formed entirely separate areas capable of holding as many people as the appropriate section of seating."

Entering the rear of the auditorium, the pit was on street level with a gentle slope towards the orchestra pit, and above, three tiers of balconies, styled as dress circle, upper circle and gallery, in all provided seating for about 3,000 people. With fronts richly decorated in colours of crimson and gold, the tiers curved and extended around the sides of the auditorium, the dress circle terminating with two boxes at either side of the proscenium. The theatre was a marvel of luxury in its appointments, these being on a grand scale. The walls were arranged in white panels, the decorative style being Corinthian and Italian, and throughout the house the new electric lights, for the first time in a Liverpool theatre, enhanced the splendour of the surroundings. The proscenium, 32ft in width was 4ft wider than any in Liverpool, and unlike almost every other theatre, the orchestra did not emerge from under the stage, a special passage having been arranged for their entrance to the orchestra pit.

With regard to internal planning, the spread of fire received the greatest possible consideration with the creation of three separate areas, divided by walls 2ft 8in thick extending all the way around from foundation to roof. The inner wall divided the auditorium from the corridors and lounges, whilst a second wall divided the lounges from the staircases and exits. In addition, over 1,000 tons of iron and concrete having been used in the walls and

floors, the building was then considered to be practically fireproof. In the emergency of a fire on the stage area, an iron curtain worked by hydraulics, the first in Liverpool, effectively shut off the stage from the auditorium.

Stated to be one of the most elaborately constructed and appointed theatres in the kingdom, the Shakespeare Theatre opened at 7.00pm on 27th August 1888, an event full of interest to Liverpool playgoers, every seat having been booked in advance. Outside, opposite the blazing starlight which advertised the entrance to the theatre, a great multitude had congregated to watch the arrivals, and feast their eyes upon the imposing facade. The opening was under the patronage of His Worship the Mayor of Liverpool, T.W. Oakshott Esq., who with his party occupied one of the private boxes. Appropriately the opening performance was of a grand Shakespearian revival of *As You Like It* in which the eminent actress, Miss Wallis (Christian name not stated) was specially engaged to play the role of saucy Rosalind. This gifted actress, long known to Liverpool playgoers was supported by a carefully selected company. The musical features of the delightful comedy were well rendered by the newly organised Shakespeare Glee Union, and despite certain shortcomings inevitable in a first performance in a new theatre, cheerfully overlooked by a good natured audience. For this fitting inauguration of Ellis Brammall's enterprise, private boxes for five cost £2, stalls, 5/-, dress circle 4/-, pit stalls 2/-, upper circle 1/6d and gallery 6d.

The Shakespeare became noted for the excellence of its pantomimes and the first of these, *The Yellow Dwarf* commenced on 22nd December 1888, but the normal policy for some years included a series of revivals by F.R. Benson and his Shakespearian company, which began with *A Midsummer Nights Dream* on 29th April 1889. Notable Shakespearian artistes subsequently appearing included Beerbohm Tree, Forbes Robertson, Sarah Bernhardt, Matheson Lang and John Hare, who took his farewell to the Liverpool stage there in 1907.

Ellis Brammall Jnr. was in control

of the theatre until in 1898, when the last performance on 2nd April was of the Robert Maneman and Louis Nethersole company's production *Blue Jeans,* then leased to Messrs. Hardie and von Leer, the theatre re-opened on 11th April with the play *A Night Out.*

In 1899 the theatre became a limited company with Mr. H.A. Bruce as managing director, who obtained a 21 year lease at an annual rental of £2,000, with an option to terminate the tenancy in 1909. The house re-opened on 14th August 1899, Christmas pantomimes continued and Boxing Night 1900 was notable for the production of *Jack and the Beanstalk,* for the cast included the well known comedian, George Robey.

Unfortunately at that time, the Shakespeare was compelled to stage some productions which did not live up to its title, and although the Carl Rosa and Doyle Carte opera companies were frequent visitors, by contrast to the established entertainment, experiments were made with different types of plays. This was instituted on 2nd September 1901 with the detective mystery play *Sherlock Holmes* by Conan Doyle,

Programme

SHAKESPEARE

THEATRE.

DESIGNED (REGISTERED No. 20001) AND PRINTED BY FRASER & WHITE, LIVERPOOL.

which was favourably received.

It transpired that the company terminated the lease considerably in advance of the agreed date, for on 18th September 1902 the theatre was for sale by auction and sold to a Mr. Temple of Liverpool. Later the proprietors were The Robert Arthur Theatres Co. Ltd., of which the managing director, Mr. Robert Arthur, was the highly esteemed lessee and manager of the Royal Court Theatre, who re-opened the Shakespeare on 6th October 1902 with the romantic comedy *Monsieur Beaucaire* for the first time in England.

The policy of the Shakespeare as principally a venue for drama was continued by Alderman W.W. Kelly, who became the lessee in 1917 following the closure during the previous year of the Paradise Street theatre which bore his name. Stage plays were presented until 1928, when the last production under the old regime, an American comedy entitled *Meet The Wife* with Constance Collier and Geoffrey Saville ended on 4th August. An immediate change was then made to variety under the control of Edinburgh Varieties Ltd., and with Alderman Kelly continuing as lessee. The Shakespeare opened on 6th August 1928 with performances at 6.45pm and 8.50pm of a variety bill headed by Dorothy Ward and Shaun Glenville, both established favourites as individual artistes of musical comedy and pantomime.

In June 1931, a new company, Liverpool Varieties Ltd., of which the managing directors were Horace H. Collins and A.W. Angus, was formed to take over and run the theatre in the position of sub lessees to Alderman Kelly.

A considerable sum was spent on extensive renovations, modernisation and re-decoration, after which the Shakespeare received a new lease of life as an up-to-date variety and revue theatre. The Company subsequently purchased it from Robert Arthur Theatres Ltd., in December 1932, after which February 1933 saw the departure of Alderman Kelly with the termination of his lease.

Whereas for nearly half a century, the leading stars of the dramatic stage had appeared at the Shakespeare, it then became Liverpool's home of variety with a

SHAKESPEARE THEATRE. LIVERPOOL

Sole Lessee & Manager, W. W. KELLY.

Bid me discourse I will enchant thine ear.

PROGRAMME

host of great stars such as Vesta Tilley, Florrie Ford, Harry Lauder, Will Fyffe, Wee Georgie Wood and Lupino Lane, also George Fromby Snr. who played the part of Idle Jack in the 1931 Christmas pantomime *Dick Whittington and his Cat.*

The great success of variety was interrupted at the time of the severe air raids on Merseyside in 1941, for although the building escaped damage, it was closed as a theatre, having been requisitioned by the corporation as a store for food. The needs for this having ceased and after re-decoration, the grand re-opening took place on 14th September 1942 with the revue, *Beauty on Duty* with performances twice nightly at 6.00pm and 8.00pm. The manager then, former actor and singer, Peter Jackson knew

variety inside out as a result of his stage experience, and although intending to remain at the theatre for only three months, found it his spiritual home, in which stroking his snuff box with his characteristic gesture, he surveyed his kingdom with pride!

The clientele increased in 1941 when two of Liverpool's other variety theatres, the Rotunda and the Metropole, Bootle were destroyed by bombs, some of their patrons then coming to the Shakespeare, to which it was reported they brought tomatoes to make known their criticisms, but were soon sorted out by Mr. Jackson. He and the Collins family kept the theatre open during some good, and some very bad times with a favoured policy of predictable entertainment for the family, comprising

dancers, jugglers, acrobats and comedians. In the post war years, this type of entertainment became increasingly more difficult to find, and completely against the Shakespeare tradition, nude shows occasionally filled in, such as *Strip, Strip, Hurrah* and *Don't Stare, its Nude,* some of which although attracting good attendances, frightened off the family trade. But they returned in large numbers for the Shakespeare's last pantomime *Red Riding Hood* starring Barbara Windsor, which commenced on 26th December 1955.

At a time of falling attendances in 1956, many were saddened to hear the announcement that this theatre of such renown was approaching the end of its days as a variety house. But there was laughter

among the tears, for on hearing of the closure, the popular comedian Dave Morris offered to make his first and last appearance at the theatre in his show *Club Night* with which it closed on Saturday, 10th March 1956.

Four Liverpool businessmen, an accountant, a cinema owner, a restauranteur, and a consulting engineer then ventured into the theatrical world, having in advance drawn up plans to convert the Shakespeare into a luxury club for members only, offering a theatre, continental cinema shows, cabaret, also dining and bar facilities. The scheme, at a cost of about £50,000, reduced the original 3,000 seating capacity to about 800, and at the rear of the stalls was constructed a projection room, from which the films were shown on to a wide screen.

In theatrical circles this was considered to be one of the most ambitious projects of its kind in the country, audiences were to be members of the club, who would pay £1/1/- joining fee, and the membership fee for one year plus the cost of a seat in the circle or stalls.

The new venture, known as the Pigalle Theatre Club, unfortunately received two immediate set backs which delayed the opening from 30th July until 6th August 1956, for apart from the fact that the builders had not quite completed their work, the biggest blow was the postponement of the world premiere of the play *The Gates of Summer*, due to the illnesses of the star, Dorothy Tutin. The Pigalle therefore opened with screen entertainment by the international award winning Italian film *La Strada* (The Road), starring Giullette Masino, Anthony Quinn and Richard Basehart.

The performances were at 6.00pm and 8.30pm, to which the general public were admitted at prices from 4/- to 6/-. Seats in the circle were bookable in advance, or patrons could pay on entering. The first stage play was a pre-London presentation of *Towards Zero* by Agatha Christie on Monday, 13th August, when seats were again available to the public for the performance at 7.00pm at 5/6d to 10/6d. This immediately conflicted with the previously announced policy of members only, and

after only six weeks, all seats for film performances, and nearly 700 of the total capacity for live entertainment were made available to the general public, indicating that considerably fewer members than anticipated had attended the performances or used the restaurant and the bar.

With regard to films, the highlights of the first months was a film each day from the National Collection during 16th-23rd September which included the silent classics *Battleship Potemkin* and D.W. Griffiths', *Birth of a Nation*.

Nevertheless in October 1956 the procedure of alternating films with live shows was abandoned so that the concentration could be on stage productions in an effort to build up a regular theatre-going membership. This did not prove successful, some of the plays were poorly attended and variety was introduced, but the club ran into difficulties when shows booked considerably in advance did not materialise. This was the case during the week before closure, and the Pigalle therefore closed on 12th May 1957, as it had opened, with a film - *Orage* featuring Charles Boyer and Michelle Morgan.

Due to dwindling audiences, the company which had tried to bring a different type of entertainment to Merseyside, went into voluntary liquidation, and the doors which, so hopefully had been opened, were again closed after only 9 months.

It is uncertain how long the theatre would have been closed, but for the visit to the Pigalle in February 1957 of American actor, producer Sam Wanamaker in a travelling company to play in *A Hatful of Rain*. At that time the Pigalle was the only theatre in Liverpool available to accommodate the company. Realising that his life's ambition was to be indentified with a particular theatre and have a permanent stage home, Mr. Wanamaker then contacted his friend of many years, Miss Anna Deere Wiman, a former American leading actress. They formed a company and bought the Pigalle, re-naming it the New Shakespeare, giving it a new lease of life when many theatres all over the country were closing down. In Mr. Wanamaker's view this was for the reason that they were open for business only three

to four hours daily, whereas his aim was to have the theatre functioning for ten hours a day with its restaurant and bars, also the continuation of the member's club from the Pigalle period to make it a centre of activity and entertainment.

Miss Wiman and Sam Wanamaker brought to the theatre people experienced in the theatrical world, Major Donald Neville-Willing, formerly general manager of the Cafe de Paris in London, was appointed to take charge of the restaurant, whilst the theatre management was in the hands of Lovat Fraser, who had held a similar position with the Old Vic Company.

Although it had been stressed that the theatre would be open to everyone, whether or not they became members of the club, it was necessary to restrict admission to them for the first two plays, since they had not been licenced by the Lord Chamberlain. The New Shakespeare Theatre opened on 31st October 1957 with a Gala Night and the first production was Arthur Miller's controversial play *A View From The Bridge* of which Sam Wanamaker was the star and the director. It was again members only during the week commencing 3rd December for the play *Tea and Sympathy* with Helen Cherry and Norman Woolland, direct from the Comedy Theatre, London.

But for the festive season family entertainment was provided by a revival of the great musical *Finian's Rainbow* which starred Shani Wallis and Bobby Howes, and ran from 26th December 1957 until 8th February 1958.

From the days as the Pigalle, film shows were continued, but on Sunday evenings only by a non-profit making organisation known as the Shakespeare Film Society, which was separate from the theatre venture. Film presentations commenced on 3 November 1957 with the English premiere of the great Russian musical *Carnival Nights* shown at separate performances 6.00pm and 8.00pm. Associate members of the theatre club, having paid a fee of of 5/-, were invited to become full members of the film society on payment of a further 2/6d. Later, a children's Saturday club was formed with performances at 11.00am.

The Shakespeare then had not only live and screen entertainment, and a restaurant, but also a permanent art gallery in the basement for which leading galleries in London gave their support by sending pictures to form special exhibitions. The venture promised to open up a new era of plays, to include during the 1958 the British premieres of *The Pinedus Affair* by Paolo Levi and *Cat on A Hit Tin Roof* by Tennessee Williams, also Sam Wanamaker appearing in two of his greatest roles in *The Rainmaker* and *The Power and the Glory*.

Despite the numerous attractions and an initial membership of almost 10,000 this surprisingly proved to be another short term venture, for after only 14 months, following the withdrawal of support by Miss Wiman in January 1959, the company was wound up with debts of £84,000. The long history of the Shakespeare as a theatre ended on 31st January 1959 with a musical play *Listen to the Wind* by Angela Ainley Jeans. The children's Saturday club also ended on that date with a performance at 11.00am of the British comedy *Hue and Cry* featuring Allastair Sim and thereafter the film shows were transferred to the David Lewis theatre.

The Shakespeare was then closed until 1963, and having been acquired by the Robley Group, a Liverpool firm of caterers, it was converted at a cost of £60,000 into a luxurious night club for cabaret and dining, also a casino with roulette and chemin-de-fer tables. All the theatre seating was removed and a new floor was constructed from the back of the original stage with an area of 400 sq. ft. to serve as a dance floor, extending across the auditorium to provide space for tables and chairs for 600 diners. The old orchestra pit was covered by a new floor for use as a dispense bar, where waiters would collect wine and dinner orders. The colour scheme was cerise and gold and illumination by subdued pink lighting.

The new enterprise opened as the Shakespeare Theatre Club on 28th October 1963, but only just over two weeks later, disaster struck during the early hours of 15th November, when a 60 minute blaze severely damaged the interior.

During the ensuing three years, the Robley Group expended £175,000 on a massive restoration scheme, which included a new system of moveable stage, three dining areas and a 60ft long bar. The atmosphere of the Victorian theatre was brought back with the restoration of the ornate embellishments of the walls and ceiling, also the re-touching and replacing in their old positions of the paintings of cherubs and cupids, whilst the smoke blue curtains set off the white and gold panelling of the walls.

Styled as the Shakespeare Casino Club, gambling facilities, roulette etc. were retained and the re-opening was on 19th September 1966 when Roy Castle and Libby Morris were among the stars of the cabaret, and an audience of about 450 dined and danced until 2.00am to a resident band.

For nearly ten more years, the Shakespeare survived through turbulent times with a succession of lessees and managers, but with little change to the basic concept of a cabaret club. Then 88 years of history cane to an end during the early hours of the rain soaked Sunday of 21st March 1976, due to a disastrous fire, which caused damage estimated at £1m after which plans to save part of the building were scrapped on advice from the city surveyors.

This latest fire reinforced the long held belief, that although the Shakespeare had been one of the most beautiful theatres in the country, it was also among the most unlucky, and it was even suggested that the place was haunted by a hoodoo, real life tragedy always hovering about its gilded walls and magnificent ceiling dome. But more practically it might be considered that since the fires had occurred after the conversion to a cabaret, the internal re-construction may have rendered the interior less safe from fire than had been provided by the original plans.

All that was left were memories from the time as a legitimate theatre with early favourites such as Sarah Bernhardt, through 70 years to the final performances of Sam Wanamaker, then as a cabaret in which appeared stars including Olivia Newton-John and Sacha Distel.

1888 THE THEATRE ROYAL/ ROYAL SUPER CINEMA, Breck Road, Anfield

The suburban theatre about 3 miles from the city was constructed to the plans of the architect, Mr. W. Redman, and provided seating accommodation for about 1,000 people, of which about 650 were in the stalls.

The opening on Christmas Eve 1888 was reported in the *Liverpool Review* as follows:-

Substantially built and tastefully decorated inside. The pit is on a level with the street, and upstairs, the dress circle, balcony and boxes are all on one floor. There are no staircases in the interior [except presumably for those to the first floor] and the several hydrants etc, make the building practically safe. From the back of the balcony the view of the stage is capitol. The fibrous plaster which embellishes the front the dress circle, the boxes and the proscenium looks remarkably well, and a pleasant relief from the ubiquitous full gold so often encountered in such places."

A fairly good audience attended for the opening ceremony. Mr. W. Wade sang the first verse of the National Anthem, and Mrs. Morteno, the second verse, the chorus joining in a military march by J.B. Richardson, musical director of the theatre. Following them, Mr. James English, the general manager concluded the inaugural ceremony with a neat and concise speech. Afterwards, Mr. Arthur Rousby's grand company proceeded with their performance of *The Bohemian Girl.*

The Theatre Royal was opened under the ownership of Mr Thomas Montgomery, who during the previous year, in partnership with James Kiernan, had instituted the conversion of the Westminster to a music hall.

After a short time, a capable stock company was engaged to perform notable plays, then came visits from touring companies, but a complete change of entertainment commenced on 3rd August 1891, when the house opened as the Theatre Royal Palace of Varieties, where among the first artistes was a then little known Liverpool comedian, Robb Wilton, who made his stage debut there, later becoming a top of the bill attraction, and during the Second World War was famous for his sketch entitled *The Day War Broke Out*.

The Royal was a variety theatre until 1906, when it reverted to legitimate theatre with up-to-date drama, played by a stock company on the popular two houses a night principle, for which the proprietor, Matthew Montogomery was commended.

A legitimate theatre until 1920, the Royal was then acquired by the W. Gordon's cinema circuit, who spent about £11,000 on transforming the building into a luxury cinema with new furnishings, decorations and lighting. The sides of the main entrance were in marble, whilst the decoration of the interior was finished off in oak panelling. Adequate internal waiting accommodation was provided, a new waiting room being constructed on the ground floor, additional to that already existing abutting the balcony.

Advertised as Liverpool's latest luxury cinema, the Royal was opened on the afternoon of Thursday, 11th November 1920, when there was a free show to guests of the directorate. They were received by the managing director of the company, Mr. W. Gordon, and secretary, R. Duncan French. The new manager was Mr. H.A. Hall, who for some ten years had been the despatch clerk for one of Liverpool's early film renters, the Weisker Bros. the occasion included a collection on behalf of St. Dunstan's Hospital, after which the film programme commenced, the feature item of this, *The Bramble Bush* starred Corinne Griffiths, a well known star of the silent screen. The cinema was open to the public in the evening with a continuous performance from 6.40pm to 10.40pm when the admission prices were 6d, 9d, and 1/3d.

The Royal survived as a cinema for over forty four years, during four changes of ownership. In 1932 it was among the halls of the W. Gordon's circuit to be acquired by the Regent Circuit Ltd., London, a subsidiary of Associated British Cinemas Ltd., created by the managing director, John Maxwell. Around May 1933 the Royal was leased to the Liverpool based Regent Enterpise Ltd., who purchased the property together with several other suburban cinemas of the Regent circuit towards the end of 1933.

In March 1938 the cinemas of Regent Enterprise were acquired in a £90,000 deal by Southan Morris Associated Cinemas Ltd., and after their period of ownership, the last proprietors of the Royal as a cinema were the Newcastle based Essoldo circuit, who took over in October 1954 and continued to operate the cinema until January 1965.

Now over 100 years of history of the Royal has been continued by its use as a bingo hall.

1890 THE PADDINGTON PALACE/ COLISEUM DE LUXE/NEW COLISEUM, Paddington

This small music hall, situated in the Edge Hill district, about one mile from the city centre, was constructed lengthwise to Paddington, with a tall gabled frontage to Upper Mason Street, a very short thoroughfare connecting with Irvine Street. It was of red brick relieved by stone with a glass canopy extending along both elevations, necessary in view of the lack of internal waiting space. The fact that it was originally an even smaller theatre than in later years is indicated by the fact that about a year after the opening in 1890, it was enlarged to accommodate an audience of 650. In the centre of the frontage, the main entrance gave access to the small rectangular foyer with stalls entrance opposite, and a white marble, metal balustraded stairway on the left, to the first floor landing, from which there was a continuation of the stairs up to the second floor entrance to the gallery at the rear of the auditorium. This was of reducing width towards the front with boxes at either side of the tall but narrow proscenium.

The theatre was opened by the

enterprising music hall proprietor, James Kiernan on 2nd September 1890, with performances at 7.00pm and 9.00pm, to which admission was 1/- and 1/6d for the best seats in the boxes, 6d in the orchestra stalls, behind which seats in the pit were 4d and up in the gallery 3d.

Although the opening of the Paddington was not advertised in the local press, and a normally reliable source of information states this as 4th September 1889, proof of the aforemention date is provided by the announcement of the second anniversary on 2nd September 1892, when the occasion was marked by an extraordinary attraction to which all patrons, past and present were invited to attend.

The continuing success of the variety performances was reported in the *Liverpool Review* of 1st July 1893, with a paragraph entitled *A Night at the Paddington* by a non-frequenter of music halls, who wrote that Mr James Kiernan was to be congratulated on the array of talent, which he had placed before his patrons. The house was packed, and in the same box as the writer was seated a city councillor, accompanied by several well known Liverpool gentlemen. Towards the end of 1893, the highly esteemed theatre manager, Mr J.S. Childs, became the proprietor of Liverpool's latest music hall, the Park Palace in Mill Street, and following his successful application for a licence, he departed from Paddington in the December of that year to commence his new venture as proprietor and manager.

Three years later, in November 1896, a new company with a capital of £90,000 in £1 shares was formed to take over from Mr. Kiernan, the Paddington Palace, the Sefton Palace, also Kiernan's United Kingdom musical and dramatic agency in a £125,000 cash and shares deal, which also included the purchase of the Tivoli Palace, Lime Street under the management of James Kiernan from the Liverpool Real Property Co. Ltd., and the Park Palace. Due to Kiernan's great success in the sphere of the music hall, it was no doubt considered advantageous that the company should be known as Kiernan's Palaces of Varieties Ltd., of which James Kiernan agreed to act

as managing director for a period of ten years, although this precluded him from taking part in any similar undertaking to that of the company in Liverpool or its immediate neighbourhood.

The Paddington house continued successfully with variety into the early 1900's, when there was a gradual change of public taste to the legitimate theatre, and accordingly the change was made in 1906 to twice nightly dramatic plays. Four years later came the end as a venue for 'live' entertainment, when the hall was leased to film exhibitors, the Weisker Bros., under whose control it became a cinema known as the Coliseum de Luxe, which opened on 2nd January 1911, advertising a gigantic programme of picture plays at a continuous performance from 6.00pm and a matinee every Saturday at 2.30pm. As at the Palais de Luxe, (formerly the Tivoli Palace, Lime Street) also run by the Weiskers as a cinema, patrons were invited to come when they liked, and stay as long as they liked, at Paddington for prices of only 2d, 4d, and 6d.

Following the departure of the Weisker Bros. c1914, the cinema continued under the control of the company, Coliseum, Liverpool Ltd. until 1926 when it was closed for some time, then acquired by the Regent Enterprise Cinema Circuit of 1-3 Stanley Street, Liverpool. The new owners carried out an extensive scheme of alterations and improvements, the principal items being the removal of the theatre boxes, and the replacement of the gallery by a waiting room at the rear, from which two entrances gave direct access to the new balcony with about 300 seats. This extended over the stalls to about half the auditorium length and increased the total seating capacity to 900.

The grand opening as the New Coliseum Picture House took place on Thursday 18th November 1926, when the company announced that the improvements had to be seen to be believed, and that the new balcony was as comfortable as any in Liverpool. There was a matinee at 2.45pm and a continuous evening performance from 6.40pm to 10.45pm for the programme of which the feature film was *His People* fea-

turing Joseph Schildkraut and all star cast. The admission prices of 1/- (balcony), 6d (stalls) and 4d (pit) were reduced to 6d, 4d and 3d at this and subsequent matinees.

The final change of ownership came in 1935 when the cinema was added to the expanding circuit of Associated British Cinemas Ltd. but at the time of decreasing audiences during the 1950s, it was among the first of their suburban cinemas to close, the date being 8th December 1956.

After several years during which the building was not used, it was demolished in May 1962.

1890
THE ROYAL MUNCASTER
THEATRE, NEW PRINCE'S
THEATRE/STRAND CINEMA,
Irlam Road

The Pennington family, who could trace their family tree to before the Norman Conquest, and for many centuries resided at Muncaster Castle, were responsible for the construction of the first purpose built theatre in Bootle, where apart from the Royal Alhambra Music Hall in Derby Road which closed c1888, public entertainment had been confined to musical evenings in local hostelries, notably, the Jawbone, the Dolphin and in the Palatine Hall, Miller's Bridge.

There was a pressing need for a permanent theatre and to fill this, Mr. Harry Pennington prepared plans for the building to be erected on waste land adjacent to the Muncaster Hotel. Construction began in 1888, but due to the death of Mr. Pennington in the August of that year, this was suspended until the following year when it was again put in hand by his sons, James and John Pennington, and completed in 1890. The building, considered to be one of the finest in the borough had an imposing facade, this was stone faced with two central entrance ways, and an exit at the extreme ends. The line of first floor windows was surmounted by arches, whilst the surfaces above and below these were relieved by panels, and the highest point of the frontage was in the form of a gable.

The interior was stated to be as brilliantly decorated as any theatre in the city, and with superb furnishings, stage arrangements and scenery. The auditorium was considered to be spacious, having a stage about 25ft in depth, and a proscenium opening 24ft wide and 20ft in height. The house was practically divided into two parts by solid brick walls, iron doors and an iron curtain, all effective in resisting fire wherever it might occur.

The ceiling of the auditorium, which rose from picturesque pilasters and arches in the walls on either side, was divided into bays by panelled beams, all gilded, and painted in such light colours that a brilliant appearance was given, these features were described as a perfect work of art. The front of the balcony, which had a graceful curve towards the proscenium, was decorated by panels and medallions, whilst the four private boxes on either side of the stage were handsomely decorated and with canopies overhead, not only formed tasteful architectural features, but added considerably to the elegance at either side of the stage. The proscenium was surmounted by a richly designed pediment panel bearing the Muncaster Coat-of-Arms.

The scenery was painted by Mr. Sam King, the well known and eminent artist of the Star Music Hall, and notable was the drop scene depicting Muncaster Castle as a reminder to the audience of the

traditions of old Bootle. From tastefully designed fittings of the ceiling and the walls a flood of light over the auditorium was shed by the gas lights, as also the stage by foot and side jets.

Messrs. Pennington, the architects were praised for the designing of one of the finest buildings in the borough, and James Pennington for his supervision of the structure throughout. It transpired however that they did not open the theatre themselves, but leased it to Messrs. H.T. Denyer and Harris Fineberg, the son of Isaac Fineberg, proprietor of the Star Music Hall. The lessees secured for the opening, some of the best variety artists in the country, in addition to several of the most popular local celebrities. The Grand Opening on 6th October 1890, was under the patronage and presence of His Worship the Mayor of Bootle, Alderman B. Cain; the Right

Honourable, the Earl of Derby, K.C., members of the Bootle Town Council, and many other distinguished persons. At 7.30pm directly after the Mayor and other V.I.P.'s were seated in the boxes, the orchestra of 15 picked musicians under the direction of Mr. Edward Jonghmans commenced the playing of the National Anthem, sung by the Liverpool Quartette. Then the overture was played as the iron curtain rose to reveal inch by inch, the magnificent back drop in old gold of Muncaster Castle. Then came the variety performance, which was enthusiastically received by the large audience which packed every part of the house. Admission was at popular prices - stage boxes 10/6d to £2/2/-, orchestra stalls 2/-, centre circle 1/6d, side circle 1/-.

The Muncaster was run as a variety theatre until 1893 when Mr. Denyer severed his connection, after which Messrs. Pennington took over the management and instituted a change to drama for three weeks of every month with variety during the fourth week, but finding that drama was then of greater appeal to the public, they decided to present theatrical entertainment only. But there were exceptions as for example the re-opening on 5th August 1901, following the installation of electric light, when the attraction was entitled *The New*

Muldoon's Picnic.

This was soon followed by the introduction of a new attraction, animated pictures, as at the Hippodrome, and other principal London Theatres, by the American Phono Bioscope Company. The presentation at the Muncaster during the week commencing 16th December 1901 was the first outside the city centre, and with sound by gramophone records, patrons were advised that they would see and hear the great artists of the time, include Vesta Tilley, Lil Hawthorne and Alec Hurley. The programme also included the great spectacular production of *The Seven Castles of the Devil* in which over 40,000 pictures were shown, also scenes of the Boer War. The prices for these were, 6d pit stalls, 1/- circle,

and 2/- orchestra stalls. Further exhibition of motion pictures were given in 1904/1905 by the New Century Animated Picture Co., three years prior to their opening of the Mount Pleasant Hall. But stage plays continued to be the principal attraction, although it was not until August Bank Holiday 1907 that twice nightly drama by a stock company was inaugurated.

Stage plays ceased in 1911 when the Muncaster came under the control of a new company, of which Dave Barnard was the director of entertainment, and J.M. Crewdson, the general manager. They reopened the theatre on 1st August 1911 with high class variety, supported by the latest motion pictures. But this short term venture ended only one year later when the

Muncaster was acquired by the highly esteemed motion picture pioneer and manager of the Sun Hall, Bootle, Mr. George Prince. A complete scheme of re-decoration was carried out, and no expense spared to make it an attractive and comfortable place of entertainment. Appropriately re-named the New Prince's Theatre, the re-opening was on 19th August 1912 when films formed the principal attraction of the performance at 8.00pm. By request the feature film was the sensational picture drama *A Victim of The Mormons* supported by the unique film *The Robbery at Old Burnside Bank.* Humour in the programme was provided by 'live' entertainment on the stage with Farrow and Fiske in a vocal pot-pourri, and Adken, the motoring ventriloquist. At this time admission prices were only 3d, 4d, and 6d.

The policy of films as the main attraction was not successful for very long, due to increased competition, for in addition to the Sun Hall, the opening of the Picture House, Stanley Road in July 1912, was followed in October by that of the district's first purpose-built cinema the Bootle Picture Palace.

By 1913 the Prince's was advertised as Bootle's now recognised variety theatre with George Prince's pictures, and continued with principally 'live' entertainment until 1921 when George Prince relinquished control. The theatre then became an addition to the Bedford cinema circuit, which controlled several cinemas in the Merseyside area, and were in a position to secure early bookings of the best films. Sparing no expense or artistic skill, the auditorium was completely re-styled for its new lease of life as a cinema to the plans of Liverpool architect, Mr. A.E. Shennan. The old theatre boxes and the circle were demolished in the conversion to a 750 seat stadium-type auditorium, all the seats being on the ground floor. These were of the tip-up type and handsomely upholstered on the floor covered by carpet, a new electric light installation was carried out, also a new heating system, and with the latest and best type of projection equipment, it was the aim of the new proprietors to show the clearest pictures in Bootle.

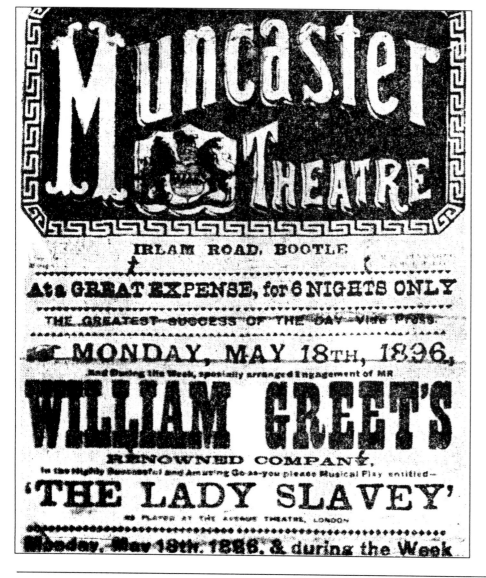

The new enterprise opened as the Strand Cinema on 19th September 1921 with a continuous performance from 6.30pm to 10.30pm, at popular prices of 5d, 9d, and 1/-. Press advertisements were worded - *"What is the Picture? Come and see, be surprised and delighted!"*

The Strand survived as a cinema for nearly 30 years, with two changes of proprietor, the first in 1928, when together with many other Merseyside cinemas, it came under the control of Gaumont British. After closure by that company in 1941 the Strand was re-opened on 3rd October by the independent company of W.J. Speakman, whose leading cinema was the Capitol, Edge Hill. Finally closing as a cinema in the late 1940s, the building was later used as a warehouse by Cork Industries Ltd., until destruction by fire on the Sunday evening of 26th July 1964.

1892
THE ROYAL PALACE OF VARIETIES, St. Mary's Road

This theatre was erected in 1892 on the site of a temporary structure, the Britannia Theatre, which was opened by a Mr J.W. Snape in 1891, prior to which, Garston was unable to boast of a permanent theatre, dramatic fare having been provided only by itinerant showmen visiting the district.

Although it had been Mr Snape's intention to build a permanent theatre, this did not materialise, but was soon followed by the construction of the Royal Palace of Varieties which was opened in 1892 under the management of Mr John Hargreaves. After being run as a variety theatre until February 1895, it was converted into a playhouse, and with a change of name to the Theatre Royal it was reopened on 3rd August 1896 by David Barnard with the play *Parson Thorn*. With plays by good companies, Mr Barnard successfully directed the theatre for several years and after he left the Theatre Royal it was converted into a billiard hall.

1892
THE ROSCOMMON MUSIC HALL/ROSCOMMON PICTURE PALACE, Roscommon Street

Named after the street, this small music hall was constructed in 1892 from two spacious dwelling houses under the supervision of a Mr. Tomkinson, who was also the proprietor of the new enterprise. But some difficulty was initially encountered with regard to obtaining a licence, for the reason that the gentlemen of the magisterial bench considered that the music hall was in bad taste, and for some time had opposed an addition to their number. A licence was however eventually granted for the opening on 16th May 1892 under the management of Mr. F.W. de Burgh. The event was attended by a reporter from the Liverpool Review, but to avoid being seen by any of the gentlemen who had opposed the granting of the licence, he crept stealthily up the steps of the front entrance, and was soon hidden away in a quiet corner, from which he could see nearly the whole of the auditorium as well as the stage. He reported that this latest of working class variety theatres was run in a business like manner, and the audience, although demonstrative were orderly. With regard to the performance, even at leading theatres, he had never seen a show more free from vulgarity, and everything objectionable than at the Roscommon. The eight items on the bill included music, singing, dancing, cycling and mimicry and concluded with a short, amusing sketch, leaving the reporter pondering for what reason the licence had been so persistently opposed.

The Roscommon seated about 600 people comfortably, and with forms on the ground floor, in excess of that number in a lesser degree of comfort at an admission price of 3d. The balcony seats at 6d were upholstered in red, and for 1/-, patrons could have a seat in one of the two boxes at either side of the stage, which presented an attractive appearance with white lace curtains. The ceiling and the walls were painted in

bright colours, and above the decorative proscenium, the Liverpool Coat of Arms occupied a central position. The orchestra pit accommodated the eight members, and the stage area of 30ft by 20ft included up-to-date requirements such as gas, lime-light and several commendable drop scenes and curtains.

With its low admission prices, for many years, the Roscommon provided 'live' entertainment at a marvellously cheap rate and ideal for the many people who found a journey to the more prestigious theatres in the city, too expensive, taking into account, fares on the tram car of about 1s 0d, for a small family in addition to the considerably higher admission prices.

ROSCOMMON MUSIC HALL,
ROSCOMMON-STREET.
Manager .. .. MR. F. W. DE BURGH.
A MODEL MUSIC HALL,
NOW OPEN. INSTANTANEOUS AND ENORMOUS SUCCESS.
MONDAY, MAY 16th, 1892, and During the Week.
The Management have secured, after severe competition the Celebrated MONOPEDES
CONWAY AND LELAND,
The originators of One-Legged Acrobats. One of the Funniest Specialities before the public.
40 Laughs in 20 Minutes !
HARRY CARSDALE,
Famous Farm Yard Mimic ! His Success in London, has been Phenomenal.
3 SISTERS PADDOCK 3
The Champion Lady Trick Bicyclists of the World.
DAVIES, THOMAS, AND HONE,
In their Side-Splitting Sketch,
OTHER CLEVER ARTISTES.
WALTER ANDREWS
NEXT WEEK.
PRICES OF ADMISSION—Boxes 1s.; Balcony 6d.; Pit 3d.
Children under Twelve Half-price.
Two Performances Nightly at 7 and 9.

Early in the present century the hall became known as King's Theatre of Varieties under the control of a lessee and the management of a Mr. Frank Calden. In 1907 music hall entertainment was continued for a short time under the direction of Mr. Frederick Willmot, who later made the change to twice nightly drama, which was then preferred by the majority of patrons. Dramatic plays were presented until 1911 by which time the growing popularity of silent films resulted in the re-opening as the Roscommon Picture Palace, then commencing a considerably longer phase in the over 60 years history of the hall. It was

KING'S THEATRE OF VARIETIES

ROSCOMMON

ROSCOMMON STREET.

Manager for the Lessee   FRANK CALDEN.

WEEK COMMENCING FEBRUARY 20. 1905.

THE CALDEN SKETCH CO.

In the highly-diverting Sketch, founded on an Incident in the late Boer War, entitled

LOVE AND DUTY!

Mr. HARRY CALDEN as "DRUMMER DOBBIE."

ROSIE LESLIE ✠ PAT NOLAN

Serio and Dancer.   Comedian.

HARRY CALDEN

Character Comedian and Dancer.

YORKE SISTERS

Vocalists and Dancers.

THE FRISCOS

Statue Dancers

---

then owned by a Mr. Tarshish, who was also the proprietor of the Adelphi Picturedrome in Christian Street, and in March 1915, the Roscommon was closed for extensive alterations to render it more suitable for the purpose of a cinema.

From about 1920 the proprietor and manager was Mr. G. Wilson, who was succeeded in 1937 by Mr. H.E. Radam, proprietor of the Doric Cinema, formerly the Westminster Music Hall. From 1940 as the Roscommon Cinema it was under the control of B. & S. Cinemas Ltd., of which the managing director was Mr. W.J. Speakman of the Capitol, Edge Hill. Their regime ended suddenly with fire damage to the auditorium during an air raid in 1941, after which the cinema was closed until 1947, then re-opened by the company, Duncan Entertainments Ltd., London W.1., follow-

ing the completion of the necessary repairs and refurbishment. At a favourable time shortly after peak cinema admission, the Roscommon opened with Western Electric sound system, and a seating capacity similar to that of the original music hall, 600 at prices from 7d to 1s 3d. Due to the rapid decrease in cinema admissions during the 1950s this was among the many closures, the final programme being screened on 13th December 1958, *White Feather* starring Robert Wagner, a CinemaScope Western, also *Overnight Haul*. The building was later used by a firm of construction engineers, after which it was demolished during a major re-development of the area.

> 1893
> THE PARK PALACE OF
> VARIETIES/PARK PALACE
> KINEMADROME/
> PARK PALACE CINEMA,
> **Mill Street**

The old coach works in Mill Street was demolished to make way for this 1,100 seat variety theatre of which the architect was Mr. J.H. Havelock-Sutton. The frontage to Mill Street was of red brick with terra cotta dressings, surmounted with a large cement panel, exhibiting in large letters the theatre name. At ground level were spaced along the well lit entrances, all with handsome doors of which the plate glass panels were draped with crimson curtains, neatly gathered in the centre. The pit was provided with two entrances and exits, each six feet wide, communicating with the street at a distance of 18ft, whilst the dress circle, stalls and gallery, each had one entrance of the same dimensions. All the vestibules were tiled with colourful tiling of a tasteful design. On the upper floors were the manager's office and the dressing rooms, which were described as the most comfortable in the provinces, being furnished with fire places and all modern sanitary accommodation. The artistes reached these from the stage door in Mill Street by a private staircase, which connected with the stage, but quite apart from the audience.

The auditorium consisted of a ground

floor and one large gallery, the former with over 600 seats divided into stalls in front and the pit behind, with an unusually sloping floor, having a gradient of seven-eights of an inch to the foot to provide a clear and uninterrupted view of the stage. The gallery seated 500 people, the two front rows of which were upholstered and styled as the dress circle. The front of the circle was decorated by fibrous plaster enrichments, and fitted with massive oval bevelled mirrors with double brass ornamental gas brackets to each, providing a brilliant lighting effect. The four private boxes were draped with electric blue plush curtains lined with plush satin and backed by white lace cur-

tains. the floors were covered with Brussels carpet upon which the seating was mahogany leather covered chairs. The box fronts were formed in fibrous plaster of Renaissance design and each box was provided with a large five-light chandelier. Decoration of the walls was by a red pattern paper above a grained wood dado, surmounted with elaborate mirrors in gilt ornamental frames, whilst the ceiling was of a most elaborate design in fibrous plaster, worked to a geometrical pattern. In the centre a large chandelier containing fifty gas burners of one hundred and fifty candle power threw a flood of light onto all parts of the auditorium.

At the front, between two boxes, the proscenium opening was 23ft in width and of a similar height, with a frame of fibrous plaster, the sides each had a massive fluted Corinthian column with ornamental cap and vase supporting a frieze and cornice of intricate design. The opening was adorned by a handsome crimson plush curtain with a deep fringe, which when drawn up from the sides by gild and red cords with massive tassels, revealed the magnificent back drop, painted by Mr. T. Holmes, scenic artist of the Shakespeare Theatre. The orchestra pit accommodated fourteen musicians, and

arranged so that they did not interrupt the audience view of the stage.

The Park Palace of Varieties was opened by the proprietor/manager, Mr. J.S. Childs on 4th December 1893 with performances at 7.00pm and 9.00pm of a variety bill which included Charles Coburn and many well known artistes of the time, reported as the strongest bill seen in Liverpool for a long time.

In 1896 the theatre was taken over by the new company, Kiernan's Palaces of Variety (Liverpool) Ltd., of which James Kiernan was the managing director, and variety entertainment continued until 1907, during which time, George Formby senior was among the many famous artistes who appeared there early in their careers. In 1904 the theatre was honoured by a Royal visitor, King Edward VII, after which the Royal Coat of Arms was installed above the proscenium.

Stage plays replaced variety in 1907, and formed the entertainment until near the end of 1908, when a Sheffield photographer who had become a cine showman, Jasper Redfern, leased the theatre, simultaneously with the Tivoli, Lime Street and opened concurrently on 21st December 1908 advertising great pictures and class vaudeville, presented twice nightly at 6.50pm and 9.00pm. The re-openings were attended by large and enthusiastic audiences, the programme was considered to be of considerable merit, and the pictures arranged by Mr. Redfern of a high class, with special mention of a film entitled A *Woman's Revenge*.

Similar entertainment was continued by this lessee until 30th June 1910, after which the exhibition of films was arranged by the Weisker Bros. coinciding with their leasing of other music halls for this purpose.

But in the following year, the proprietors, Kiernan's Palace of Varieties, sold the theatre to the Dunn family, and with Peter Dunn as managing director commenced in 1911 the Park Palace's new lease of life as a cinema for little short of 50 years. Then renamed the Park Palace Kinematodrome, for a short time films were supported by variety acts, but later, during the 1920s as the Park Palace it was pictures only accompanied by

a seven piece orchestra. Then on 8th January 1930, the talkies arrived with the installation of Western Electric sound system, after which the orchestra was no longer required.

After the death of Peter Dunn in 1934 the family continued to run the cinema, and in 1941, his daughter Sheila Dunn, became the managing director, under whose control the Park Palace survived through the war years, and to near the end of the 1950s when decreasing attendances forced the closure on 11th March 1959. It was observed that television and bingo had achieved, in that which Hitler had failed during the World War II, to close, the 66 years' old Park Palace.

1897
LYRIC THEATRE,
Everton Valley

This was, for a suburban theatre at that time, a larger than average building, with an auditorium comprised of stalls, boxes, circle and gallery in which an audience of 2,000 could comfortably be seated. Erected on the quite steep gradient of Everton Valley, near to its junction with Walton Road, the Lyric was the enterprise of Ellis Brammall, Jnr., who inaugurated the Shakespeare Theatre in the city.

The tall, imposing frontage of terracotta brick work with stone reliefs in the form of pilasters and festoons, included at

LYRIC SUPER - CINEMA.
EVERTON - VALLEY.
Extensively Renovated Throughout.

GRAND REOPENING TO - DAY,
MONDAY.
Comfort, with Perfect Projection.
MATINEE DAILY at 3. CONTINUOUS from 6.30.

WEAVERS OF LIFE,
A Story, showing how Love and Devotion are more
than Wealth and Position.
SUPPORTED BY AN ALL-STAR PROGRAMME

ORCHESTRAL ACCOMPANIMENT EVERY
EVENING.

POPULAR PRICES. bmb

ground level, three wide arched entrance ways, each with glass panelled doors to the large foyer, in which was a handsome, carved oak centre piece, and an electric light candelabra. At first floor level, the exterior featured five, tall arched windows, surmounted by a central panel bearing the theatre name. This was flanked on either side by a pediment, whilst a gable in the centre formed the highest point of the frontage. The auditorium was described as attractive, being rich in crimson velvet, polished mahogany, cream and gold adornments, and the ceiling dotted all over with electric lights was a beautiful piece of ornamentation. The artistically designed proscenium was flanked on either side at dress circle level by curved fronted boxes with elegant plush drapes.

The Lyric Theatre was opened on 26th December 1897 by the lessee and manager, Mr. H.C. Arnold with performances at 2.00pm and 7.30pm of the pantomime, *Blue Beard* written by J.H. Wolfe. The boxes could be booked in advance for 21/- whilst in the other parts of the house, the orchestra stalls were 2/-, circle 1/6d, pit 1/- and the gallery 6d. As at the majority of theatres, evening patrons entering one hour before the performance, by the early doors, obtained a better selection of the unbooked seats on payment of an extra 3d or 6d.

Having made his first appearance at the Liverpool Amphitheatre in the autumn of 1871, then a member of the famous Rotunda stock companies, later touring with his own company, Mr. Arnold was a well known actor. After touring for several years, he decided to open his own theatre, and chose the Lyric, which from the outset was considered a credit to himself and his native city. With the exception of a pantomime every Christmas, Mr. Arnold ran the Lyric for over five years as a venue for drama, securing the best talent, but with the addition of the theatre to the Barrasford Tour (Circuit) of music halls, proprietors of the newly opened Royal Hippodrome, the Lyric became a popular twice nightly variety theatre from Easter Monday 1903.

For many years the Lyric presented variety, then occasional plays followed by a considerable period of closure before its addition to the W. Gordon's cinema circuit, which controlled several Liverpool suburban cinemas including the nearby Garrick, Westminster Road. After extensive renovation and redecoration, the grand reopening as the Lyric Super Cinema took place on the 19th September 1921. Comfort with perfect projection at popular prices was advertised. In accordance with normal future policy,

there was a matinee at 3.00pm and evening performances continuous from 6.30pm to 10.30pm. The feature film *Weavers of Life* was supported by an all star programme, with orchestral accompaniment in the evenings. The venture however, proved to be short lived, for no application was made for the renewal of the cinematograph licence, which expired on 31st October 1924.

The theatre was then available for rent and later came under the control of J. Leslie Greene, who was well known in the theatrical and kinematograph worlds, being chairman of the Liverpool Cinematograph Exhibitors Association, also managing director of the company which had recently taken over the Metropole Theatre, Bootle.

The Lyric was redecorated, refurnished and equipped with a new central heating system for the reopening as a theatre on 28th December 1925, with performances at 6.40pm and 8.50pm of the sensational revue success *There You Are Then!* attended by a large, enthusiastic audience, who welcomed with delight the return of 'live' entertainment. This was described as a merry affair throughout with droll comedian, George Mayfield receiving excellent support from the talented company, and one of the most acceptable features was the Alabama Syncopated Orchestra of skillful musicians, who brilliantly played the latest dance tunes.

It is recorded that in 1927, the later to be well known comedian, Ted Ray, whose real name was Charles Olden, appeared at the Lyric for £7.00 per week, and there was also an appearance of the sister of comedian Stan Laurel.

The Lyric had a comparatively short life as a theatre, its closure being as a result of a report by the Liverpool Fire Brigade which stated that a fire hazard existed due to unsatisfactory exits. This resulted in closure on 19th November 1932, with the last of a successful series of revues by Fred. D. Nielson - *Laugh and Risk It.*

The building was later used as a warehouse and destroyed by enemy action in 1940. Although the site was subsequently cleared, the lower portion of the rear wall of the theatre remained for many years, providing a memory of the

Lyric with the still clearly visible painted sign - "6.40 Twice Nightly 8.50".

1902 THE ROYAL HIPPODROME, West Derby Road

This was the first of a circuit of fourteen music halls called Hippodrome which were opened within a period of four years from 1902 by Thomas Barrasford, the northern variety entrepreneur, who challenged the supremacy of the Moss & Stoll Empire theatres. The site on the West Derby Road, near to Brunswick Street, had since 1876 been occupied by Hengler's Grand Cirque, an area of 20,000 square feet with total accommodation for 4,500 persons. The proprietor and director was Albert M. Hengler, and the closure on the Saturday evening of 9th February 1901 was the end of a long and brilliant chapter in the history of the circus.

After remaining unoccupied for several months, the building was acquired by Thomas Barrasford as managing director for the syndicate, Liverpool Hippodrome Co. Ltd. and in February 1902, except for portions of the four main walls, the site was cleared for the erection of the new theatre, the Royal Hippodrome, by the three hundred strong workforce of Liverpool contractors, William Tomkinson & Co. who completed the work in the short time of about six months. The new building of hitherto unequalled size and beauty reflected great credit upon the architect, Bertie Crewe and A. Skelmerdine, brother of the city surveyor. The former, a man of wide experience in the designing of music halls in the Style of Louis XV, was also the architect of the later Barrasford Hippodromes.

The principal elevation of the building was set quite far back from the main road, with architectural features of five tall first floor windows, set within stone arches, whilst above, several small windows were surmounted by an attractive stone balustrade along the apex. The main entrance on West Derby Road, between a bank on the left and shops on the right, fronted a single storey gabled extension between the other properties to provide a long vestibule, of which the mosaic floor, the pride and joy of Albert Hengler, had been left from the old building at his request. The entrance, surmounted by an arch and the Royal coat of arms, was fitted with a glass canopy, supported by iron columns, which extended to near the pavement edge. Constructed of concrete and iron, with floors resting upon iron supports on the cantilever system, the theatre was among the largest in the provinces, with accommodation for about 4,000 people and a seating capacity of 3,500, of which the gallery seated about 1,500 without crushing, and the pit about 1,000.

The auditorium was described as pretty and ornate with fine decorations by an abundance of carved fibrous plaster designs in prevailing colours of cream and grey with gold enrichments. The most outstanding feature of the decorations was the ceiling, from which hung handsome electric pendants, the large dome being adorned by a work of art on canvas, emblematical of music and the arts, by the famous artist Mr Secard of London, who painted Cupids resplendent upon beds of clouds. Further examples of his artistry were to be found above the proscenium, with five extremely artistic paintings depicting the Five Senses, and the adjoining two attractive paintings of Arcadian beauty. The 40ft wide proscenium had a base of marble and above, the intricate fibrous plaster designs of the opening were in colours of yellow, red and gold, and in front of this was the orchestra pit for twenty five musicians. The stage, 90ft in width and 40ft deep, with a height to the flies of 27ft 6in was fitted with an up-to-date fireproof curtain. To this, from practically any part of the square shaped auditorium, it was claimed that the line of vision was uninterrupted. Although gas provided the secondary lighting, the theatre was lit principally by electricity, which also provided illumination for the latest novelty, animated pictures shown by a projector, housed in a steel fireproof chamber to the rear of the circle. The plans also included lounge and refreshment buffets, to be run with a teetotal policy.

The Grand Opening of the Royal Hippodrome on 4th August 1902, with a policy of twice nightly variety performances at rock bottom prices, of which Thomas Barrasford was a pioneer, marked an epoch in Liverpool music hall history. The event created enormous interest among the citizens of Liverpool, proof of which was evident by the long queues of patient people outside the theatre, who seemed to have been waiting for much of the day for admission to the initial performances.

Immediately prior to the performances at 7pm and 9pm, the large orchestra conducted by Mr E. Walker struck up with the *National Anthem* and Lucy Clarke, the Irish contralto began with the well known words. These were soon caught up by the standing audience, who were unanimous in the performance of the anthem, after which the variety show of ten acts was headed by the expensively engaged acrobats, the Six Sisters Daineff. The top price of admission was 2/- for a seat in the boxes, whist a seat in the orchestra stalls was 1/-, the circle 6d and the gallery 2d.

Mr Barrasford's spirited enterprise and excellent catering were a great success, the Hippodrome providing such powerful competition to Moss & Stoll's Empire Theatre, that Barrasford's rivals decided on the building of an even larger theatre in close competition on West Derby Road, the Olympia which it transpired, failed to approach the success of the Hippodrome.

After the death of Thomas Barrasford in 1910, control of the company passed to South of England Hippodromes Ltd. in accordance with his prior arrangement with their managing director, Walter de Frece, whose circuit plus the larger Barrasford halls, including the Liverpool Hippodrome, in 1914 made up a total of eighteen properties, of what was then known as the Variety Theatres Controlling Company, then at it's maximum number.

Walter de Frece, husband of Vesta Tilley, the famous music hall artist, was knighted for his services to British entertainment in 1919, after which he resigned his position as managing director to enter politics. He was succeeded by Charles Gulliver, who had replaced Sir Walter Gibbons as head of the London Theatres of Variety. The Hippodrome then became one of the Gulliver circuit theatres until March 1928, when in a £5m countrywide deal which included the Liverpool Rialto and many other cinemas in the Merseyside area, the new proprietors of the Hippodrome were the General Theatre Corporation, under whose control it later became a Gaumont British cinema.

Variety continued for a further three years, the final performance being on Saturday 20th June 1931, when there were tears and sighs and standing room only, as the crowds came for the last time to admire and cheer their favourites at the end of an era. Heading the bill was Harry Champion with his rollicking choruses, and Vesta Tilley singing *Waiting at the Church,* supported by a great cast of artists of the time. The enthusiastic support for this final show gave the impression that variety could have lasted for another thirty years, but then owned by a cinema circuit, with sound films having become the popular entertainment attraction, the change to a cinema was complete and no further live entertainment was seen at the Hippodrome.

The theatre was closed for one month for the conversion, which resulted in a great reduction in the seating capacity to 2,100, due to increased spacing between rows of the stalls and circle seats. The gallery seating remained unchanged for occasional use if necessary and above this floor, built into the roof, a projection room about 18ft square was constructed. A British Acoustic sound system was installed and due to the steep angle of projection, the Kalee machines were set at an angle of 26 degrees.

For the opening as a cinema on 20th July 1931 the feature film was the first Liverpool showing of *Dracula* starring Bela Lugosi, supported by a second feature, *We Dine at Seven,* featuring Herbert Mundin. In accordance with normal future policy, performances were continuous throughout the day, and admission prices from 5d to 1/3d.

The Hippodrome survived as a cinema for nearly forty years, although at the time of decreasing cinema attendances

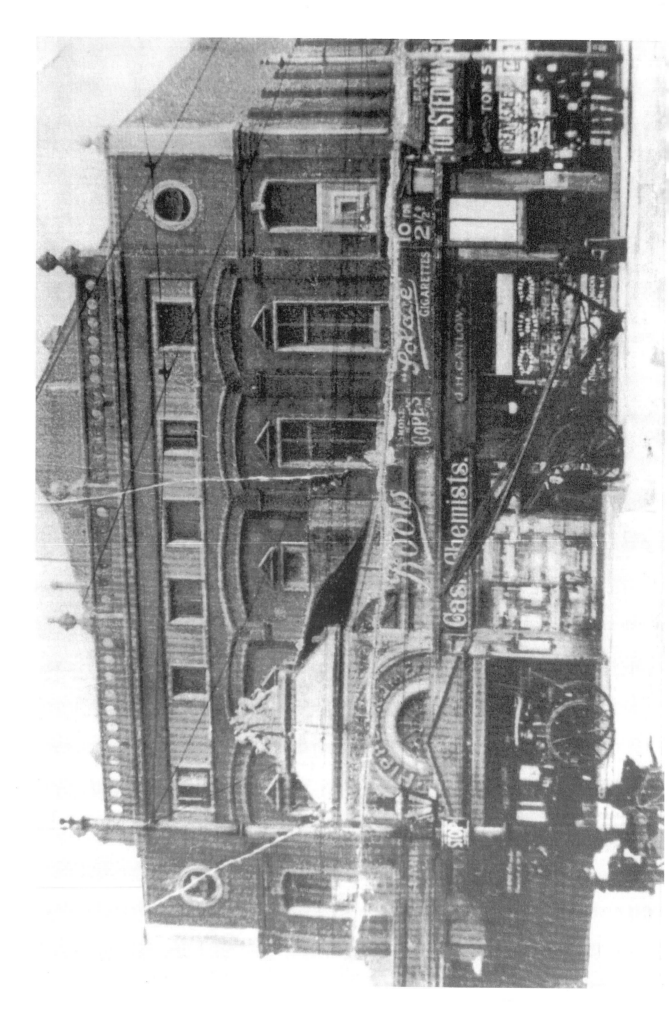

from the mid 1950s, had the disadvantage of excessive size, seating capacity and consequently high running costs. Although by the summer of 1967 no cinemas remained in close competition, admissions again decreased when many local residents left the district due to the major redevelopment scheme, which included the widening of West Derby Road. In these circumstances the proprietors, then the Rank Organisation, closed the Hippodrome on 16th May 1970 with the programme, *Winning,* starring Paul Newman and *The Pipeliners.* The building was not subsequently used and for many years lay derelict until demolished in 1984.

1905
OLYMPIA THEATRE,
West Derby Road

Having been erected on the site formerly occupied by the Liverpool Licensed Victualler's Asylum of 1852 for necessitous widows and orphans of deceased members, brought forth the comment from the humourists of the district that the proprietors, Moss Empires Ltd. must have been mad to institute the building of a theatre so close to Barrasford's Hippodrome, especially since they also controlled the Empire Theatre in the city centre. However, the new venture was in accordance with their formerly stated policy, to build a larger and finer theatre, wheresoever, in direct opposition to their rival. Although it did not prove to be anything like so successful as they would have wished, the Olympia was then Great Britain's largest variety theatre and architecturally among the most magnificent. In later years, it has been described as an Edwardian jewel which the city should conserve, but ironically, the fact that it continued to exist in the last decade of the century is due to attractions other than theatrical and into the 1990s as a venue for bingo, which to date has provided the last opportunity to view the magnificent auditorium.

The Olympia was designed by the great theatre architect, Frank Matcham, who chose for the facade the free Italian Renaissance style in red pressed brick and stone dressings. The great width of the three storied frontage consisted of a long splayed section at either side of the straight centre, which at ground level was allocated to the four arches of the main entrance surmounted by a glass canopy. Directly above, the construction was entirely of stone, with a grouping on two floor levels incorporating the principal windows, with columns supporting an entablature. Over the coping a glass sunray feature was surmounted by a massive central tower with mechanical revolving sign above, and flanked on either side by small minarets, whilst panels above the coping of the splayed sections of the frontage, displayed in large letters the theatre name.

The auditorium was a masterpiece of elaborately carved plasterwork in colours of cream, blue and red relieved by gold. The stalls floor included sixteen rows of comfortable tip-up seats and at the rear, a cinematograph room was a permanent structure and feature of the planning. On either side of this were ten private boxes and a further two at either side of the stage, with Indian style canopies, fitted with scarlet plush drapes of a similar style. The side elevations on the dress circle and balcony levels were decorated by ornamental pilasters and Indian panelling, between which full length carved elephantine figures supported the ceiling trusses.

Appropriate to the architectural style, the tableaux curtains, as all the curtains and drapes, were of brilliant oriental scarlet plush, enriched by wide embossed upright bands and further ornamented at the base and sides by borders of applique design in deeper shades of crimson and gold, and finished with a massive silk fringe, three feet deep. Surmounting this, the proscenium valance was prettily draped and embellished with applique designs in gold and silver, also scarlet plush on a brocaded background.

The stage, second in size only to that of London's Drury Lane Theatre, incorporated a distinctly novel feature, in that by means of hydraulic power, at the pull of a lever, the 42ft wide arena disappeared from sight in 20 seconds and replaced by a huge tank containing 80,000 gallons of water with fountains, camouflaged to resemble a lake for aquatic displays. Since the circus was also to be among the attractions, a solid brick and concrete pit was constructed below the stage, which housed the lion's cages and accommodation for the horses etc. and in the auditorium the orchestra pit and the first dozen or so rows of seats were removeable to make way for the sawdust ring.

The vast auditorium comfortably seated an audience of 3,750 in stalls, boxes, dress circle, upper circle and gallery, and for their egress the architect provided no fewer than thirty six exits. However, despite the numerous attractions offered in such elegant surroundings, and the eagerness of the proprietors to make the Olympia Liverpool's leading theatre, it soon transpired that the problem was how to get people into,

rather than out of the theatre.

Nevertheless the Olympia opened successfully on Easter Monday 24th April 1905 with performances at 6.50pm and 9pm of the spectacular equestrian review, *Tally Ho,* direct from the London Hippodrome and starring the famous George Formby senior, which ran for four weeks, with pictures on the Bioscope as an added attraction. Stated to be as low as the standard of the performance was high, private boxes to seat four were at 5/- and 7/6d, Arena Stalls 1/6d, Orchestra Stalls 1/- (all numbered and bookable in advance without extra charge), Grand Circle 6d, Balcony 4d and Gallery 2d (3d on Mondays, Saturdays and holidays).

During its twenty years as a theatre, the Olympia presented every conceivable type of entertainment - circus, water pageants, opera, ballet, music hall, pantomimes, films and even boxing, with exhibition bouts

including the great Jack Johnstone. Among the famous artists in the various entertainments were ballerina Pavlova, Seymour Hicks, Ethel Levy, Lawrence Irving, Wilkie Bard, George Formby senior and the famous actress Sarah Bernhardt, who gave her last Liverpool performance at the Olympia.

A noteable change from live entertainment was presented between 24th April and 20th May 1916 when the Olympia became entirely a cinema with a special presentation of D.W. Griffiths *The Birth of a Nation* accompanied by the symphony orchestra of thirty six players. The three hour performance commenced at 2.15pm and 7.15pm with prices ranging from 6d in the gallery to 21/- in the stalls.

Later in an attempt to improve attendances Moss Empires appointed one of their most astute managers, Pierre Cohen to take charge, and cine-variety was among the

attractions. However, in 1925 the theatre was acquired by Savoy Cinemas Ltd., then the latest organisation to commence big scale cinema operations. The last performances as a theatre under the old regime were given on Saturday 7th March 1925 when the British National Opera Company gave performances of *Faust* at 2pm and *Tannhauser* at 7pm.

The Olympia was then closed for three weeks for the work of conversion to a super cinema, with seating capacity reduced to 3,400 in re-arrangement of the sight lines to the new screen. Considered to be one of the finest in the country, this was set at a distance of 30ft from the first row of the stalls. The latest Ross projectors were installed for the projection of the silent films, which were to be accompanied by the orchestra of 24 musicians under the leadership of C. Kottaun, late of the Oxford Theatre, London. The new decorations were on novel lines giving the impression that the colours were merging together to produce a scheme of indefinable quality with a setting sun effect. The new proprietors announced that the excellent stage facilities would continue to be used with 'live' entertainment as a prologue to the latest and best film productions.

Continuing under the management of Pierre Cohen, the re-opening on 30th March 1925 was as the Olympia Super Cinema, with the inaugural attraction *The Thief of Baghdad* featuring Douglas Fairbanks senior. Supporting films were - *A Society Knockout* with Jack Dempsey, also the Grand National and special events, whilst 'live' entertainment was provided by the celebrated operatic star, Frank Mullings. Admission prices were, back stalls 1/6d, grand circle and stalls 1/-, upper circle 6d and balcony 4d to the continuous performance from 2.30pm to 10.30pm.

Nearly four years later, the Olympia reached a peak of success as a cinema, being the first in Liverpool, and only the fourth outside London, to be equipped for the permanent exhibition of sound films or the *talkies* as they were known. The first of these, *The Singing Fool*, starring Al Jolson opened on 11th January 1929 and ran for seven weeks until 30th March with separate

performances at 2.00pm, 4.00pm, 6.00pm and 8.00pm, and seat prices from 6d to 3/6d. Then for the first time, the enormous seating capacity was insufficient to accommodate the large crowds who rushed to see the film. Queues were so long that those near the back were out of sight of the theatre! The absence of advance booking was therefore the subject of comment.

The Olympia and the Prince of Wales cinema in the city were acquired in 1930 by Associated British Cinemas Ltd., these being the first of the company's cinemas in the Liverpool area. Although normally presenting the same feature film, at the Olympia, variety acts were an added attraction

during the early thirties.

Following the addition to the circuit of numerous other cinemas in the Liverpool area, A.B.C. closed the Olympia on 25th March 1939, then showing a double feature programme, *Stablemates* starring Wallace Beery, also *Girl's School*, 'live' entertainment having ceased.

The building was used as a naval depot during World War II and in March 1948 it was acquired from A.B.C. by Mecca Ltd. who instituted extensive alterations for the conversion into the Locarno ballroom, which opened in 1949. A small semi-circular bandstand was constructed against the rear wall of the stage, with the former stalls area becoming the ballroom floor, and the cinema projection room under the principal balcony at the rear was demolished. A glass-fronted room on the main balcony was used to house spotlight and electrical control gear. The ballroom was open for 15 years, after which the Olympia was again extensively altered for the opening in August 1964 as a luxury bingo casino in which the decorations were restored to their former glory.

Due to decreasing attendances, bingo ceased in August 1982, when the building was advertised for sale, but the fact that a purchaser was not found during the ensuing four and a half years, and the £60,000 per annum cost of maintaining the disused property, prompted Mecca to re-open with bingo. Great efforts were made to bring the building back into use while preserving its unique character. £150,000 was spent on skilful repairs to the elaborate internal plasterwork including the famous elephant heads, new bingo equipment was installed, and since only the stalls and the first floor balcony were to be used, the upper levels were curtained off to contain the heating.

The re-opening of the Olympia for bingo on 9th April 1987 commenced with the swirl of kilts and the skirl of bagpipes when the Wirral Pipe Band marched from the back of the circle down to the stalls and around the auditorium to the front of the stage, where they played several tunes. The official opening was performed by the principle guest of the evening, Danish born Liverpool footballer, Jan Molby, who cut a

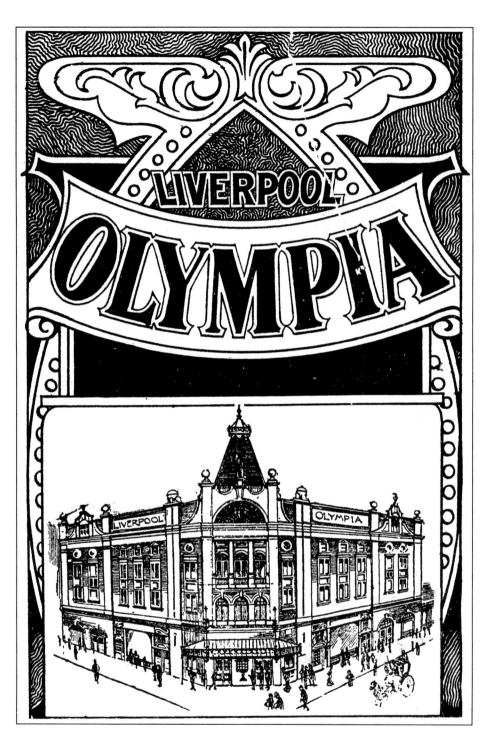

1906
THE DAVID LEWIS
THEATRE,
Great George Place/Upper
Parliament Street

This small rectangular theatre with centre and side balconies and seating accommodation for 540, was constructed in 1906 within the David Lewis building, a large five storey, stone-faced edifice, flanked by a tower at each end. This was in its own grounds, developed with railed garden areas and paths leading to the imposing arched main entrance flanked by columns.

Its origin was the David Lewis Trust, formed in 1893 to give effect to the generous intentions of philantropist, David Lewis, the founder of Lewis's stores, whose aim was to provide the population of one of Liverpool's poorest areas with opportunities for social life and recreation at affordable prices.

The theatre was intended primarily as a music hall for men using the David Lewis Hotel and Club, but it was a large, and even in those days, elaborate structure, and it soon became apparent that the restriction of use to its original purpose would be bad economy. The then warden, Mr. (later Sir) Frederick Marquis therefore made arrangements with local amateur societies for the development of dramatic entertainments, for which with regard to stage and general equipment, the theatre became very satisfactory as the home of amateur dramatic work. This achieved the aim of the committee to bring good drama within reach of the poorest, sometimes at prices from 2d to 1/-. A number of experiments of considerable importance were made, societies being invited to give performances free of expense to themselves, later hiring the hall for the presentation of plays to their own members. The Tuesday and Saturday evening shows at considerably reduced prices continued with great success for a number of years, and the Sunday evening concerts provided one and half hours good music for 2d, with an uninterrupted run into the thirties. Another attraction which ran for a

ceremonial red ribbon across the stage after an enthusiastic reception.

It transpired however, that this time bingo was to be a short lived attraction, and for the reason of low attendances, the Olympia closed after only about 12 months. Since April 1990 under the ownership of Silver Leisure Ltd,. proprietors of the adjoining Grafton Ballroom, the theatre remains closed to date with an uncertain future.

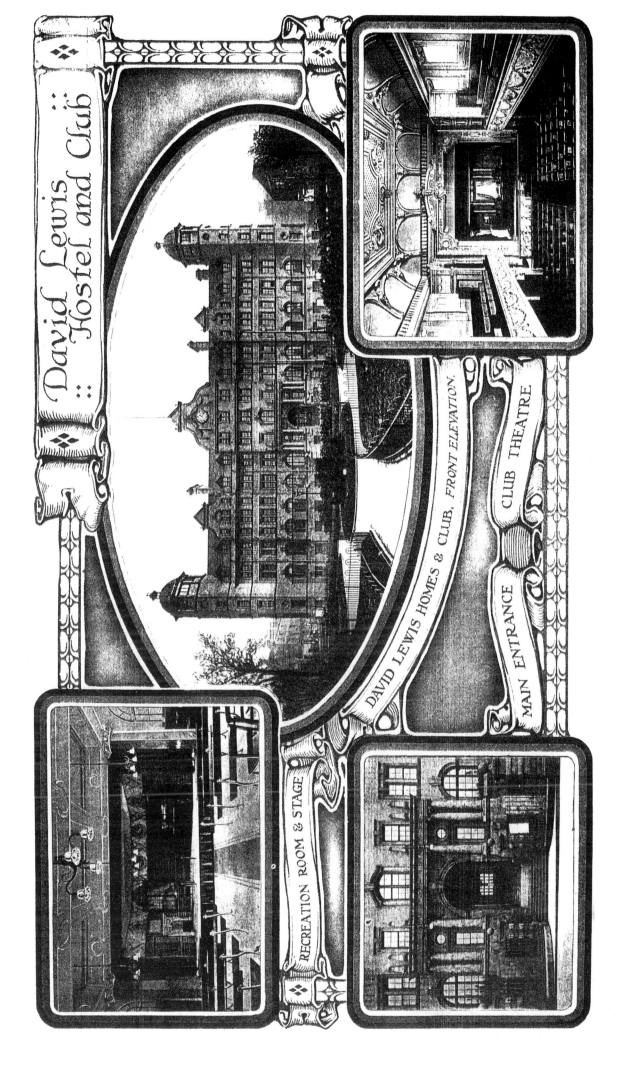

David Lewis
:: Hostel and Club

DAVID LEWIS HOMES & CLUB. FRONT ELEVATION.

CLUB THEATRE

MAIN ENTRANCE

RECREATION ROOM & STAGE

number of years was a series of amateur operatic productions, the inspiration of a Mr. John Tobin.

From the beginning of 1926 for about seven years, the David Lewis was particularly associated with the national drama festivals, but then diminished in local amateur affairs. Despite alternative schemes it was not until the appointment in December 1933 of Mr. Harold King as the new warden of the David Lewis club that a solution was found. The scheme sponsored by Mr. King was that amateur societies should be responsible for a regular repertory of plays, each society playing two or three evenings per week. At that time the governors of the institution approved the formation of a committee for the management of the theatre under the Chairmanship of Mr. Rex A.L. Cohen, one of their own number, who were men prominently associated with the amateur theatre.

In May 1934, the first part of a four year plan of alterations and improvements was announced, to be done gradually as funds became available, and by which it was hoped that the theatre would be brought entirely up-to-date. A wall erected between the pillars in the existing entrance hall, provided a separate foyer for the theatre with a new booking office, a refreshment room and new toilets. On the right-hand side, a continuation of the wall enclosed the staircase to the first floor foyer with re-conditioned refreshment room for patrons of the balcony. These alterations effectively enclosed the theatre from the other activities of the hostel and the club. At the stage end, dressing room accommodation was increased and some re-decoration was carried out to the auditorium, which for one of its size had many architectural features. The proscenium was of classic style with attractive carved designs and supporting a vase at the highest central point, and from the auditorium walls extended the deep cornice and balustrade above. All around this was surmounted by a curved, panelled section which extended up to the principal straight centre of the high ceiling. From this were sus-

pended several chandeliers, the largest from the central panel to a lower level by a very long chain.

The shallow balcony at the rear opposite the stage, and the straight extensions along either side were supported by light iron columns, the fronts decorated by an abundance of plaster mouldings, including festoons terminated with an arched fronted box flanking the stage. The upper part of the side walls was decorated by elegant panels, between which, pilasters with carved capitals extended up to the cornice.

The policy of the management was to make the building a centre for the amateur theatre in the district and improving it so that it might provide all the amenities to be found in a commercial theatre.

The increasingly important part which the amateur theatre was taking in the commercial life of Merseyside was emphasised when the David Lewis re-opened on the evening of 12th October 1934 in the presence of the Lord Mayor and Lady

Mayoress, Mr. & Mrs. G.A. Strong. The large audience included many civic leaders and representatives of most the Liverpool Amateur Dramatic Societies, for the performance of *The Merry Death* described as a macabre little play by Evreinov.

By 1936 the David Lewis Theatre was the producing home of a number of first rate amateur societies, offering facilities by which poor and struggling companies could present their productions under professional conditions. At this time, to the membership was added a member who was particularly interested in films, for the showing of which the theatre had been equipped in the early days of motion pictures. The old apparatus was then discarded and replaced by two of the latest sound film projectors, thereby also providing a well equipped centre for experimental film work of all kinds. During the previous two years the possibility of co-operation with the valuable work of the Merseyside Film Institute Society had been explored and resulted in the society holding six evenings at the David Lewis during the 1936/37 season.

A large number of persons connected with film and stage work in Liverpool were invited to the opening night on 18th September 1936, when the programme was comprised of several films including John Grierson's latest work for the G.P.O. unit, *The Fairy of The Phone* also a Gaumont British instructional film *Coal,* a Mickey Mouse cartoon and one or two other shorts. Later in the evening the Playgoers Club presented *The Devil among the Skins,* the production which had recently toured in Germany at the invitation of the British Drama League.

The history of the David Lewis would not be complete without reference to its indefatigable stage manager, Mr. George Creed, who was associated with the theatre from its foundation, for it was due to his utmost enthusiasm and genius in the practical work of the theatre, that progress up to that time had been made.

Wartime brought great changes, for in November 1940, the David Lewis became the new Garrison Theatre with club and canteen facilities where the troops ran their own variety shows, boxing tourna-

ments, and various other events, the cost of re-adapting receiving generous support from the Lord Mayor's War Fund. During the war the doors did not close and over 1,300 different entertainment programmes ranged from symphony concerts, operas and plays to boxing and variety concerts. At the time of severe air raids on Merseyside, the May Blitz in 1941, this large building became a community centre where food and shelter was provided for 2,500 homeless people.

After notable service both to the armed forces and civilians during the war, the David Lewis reverted to a peace time basis in 1945, when a new committee was formed under the Chairmanship of Sir Andrew McNair. The governors believed that the function as a Community Centre should be retained, to provide all social work from the running of a day nursery to caring for the aged.

At the end of the 1950s, the theatre in its present form, was considered as more suitable to the generation of 50 years previously than to the young people of that time. The governors of the David Lewis Hotel and Club Association announced that the theatre was to be remodelled at a cost of £5,000 for the additional purpose of a dance hall. The existing raked floor was replaced by a level sprung floor of maple wood to accommodate 200 dancers, but this did not affect the use as a theatre, for which 296 movable seats were provided. The fixed seating in the balcony was retained, giving a total seating capacity of 470, and the under side of the balcony was boarded in to form a false ceiling in which recessed lighting was fitted. The auditorium was entirely redecorated in a pastel colour scheme of blues, greys and off white with contrasting maroon and cyprus green. In addition to the dual purpose of theatre and dance hall, it was claimed that having installed modern cinema equipment for the showing of normal and wide screen films, the facilities in this respect were comparable with those of any local cinema.

The newly re-styled and redecorated David Lewis Theatre/Ballroom was given an informal send off on the evening of 10th October 1960, when the Chairman of Governors, Mr. Leslie S. Cohen welcomed

members of the governing board and representatives of organisations dealing with youth activities. During the evening the new floor was tested by members of the youth club, who gave an exhibition of 'jive' dancing.

The David Lewis remained open until 1977, when due to severe financial losses, funds were not available for the carrying out of the necessary work in connection with health and safety regulations. But apart from this threat to it's future, the building was on the route of a proposed inner motorway, and had since the mid-sixties been under threat of demolition, this being its ultimate fate in November 1980.

The David Lewis Association Club continues to date at premises in Stanhope Street.

1908
PAVILION THEATRE,
Lodge Lane

Known throughout Liverpool as the 'Pivvy' this variety theatre still holds many happy memories for the city's older generation, although few will now remember the proprietor, William Henry Broadhead, who died in 1931, when a special train took more than 400 mourners from the city to his funeral in Blackpool. Broadhead was responsible for the building and the opening of a chain of theatres throughout the North-West, and often as in the case of the Pavilion, he bought homes nearby to provide accommodation for the staff. It appears that the venture came as a surprise locally, for at the time when construction commenced in 1907, it was not generally known that the construction of this exceptionally fine theatre had been contemplated.

In a situation about one and a half miles from the city centre, the shape of the site area and the existence of shops fronting onto Lodge Lane, necessitated the construction of two elevations. At the extreme left was the frontage to the road and areas leading to the principal elevation, the audito-

rium, lengthwise to Lodge Lane, at the rear of the shops and separated from those properties by a small road. The tall frontage included the almost full width main entrance surmounted by a canopy which gave access to the foyer with 'island' pay-box/booking offices, opposite to these was sited the main staircase to the circle lounge and entrances, whilst at ground level on the right-hand side were located the entrances at the rear of the stalls.

Described as among the finest in the country, the auditorium originally had a seating capacity of about 2,500 in the parts designated as private boxes, numbering eight, stalls, pit, circle and balcony. The latter two floors with eleven rows of seats in each, were partly supported by iron columns, and had a wide curve which terminated in a composition of four boxes on either side of the stage, two at each level stepped down from the balcony fronts. Dividing the boxes, giant pilasters carried on large scrolled brackets, projected from the side walls of the stalls. The box fronts and the lower balcony front were decorated by large cartouches, and the upper balcony front by repeated festoons between cartouches. The boxes were widely angled away from the richly framed rectangular proscenium, which although 36ft in width, appeared narrow in relation to the great width of the auditorium. The polygonal ceiling was carried on very deep coves above the boxes and the proscenium and decorated by large panels. The stage with a depth of 38ft was sufficiently large for all forms of theatrical and variety settings, and the dressing room accommodation of a standard to please the most fastidious of artists.

The completeness of the planning was typified by the most elaborate engine room with three independent electricity generators to preclude the possibility of light failure, and if all else failed, gas lights throughout provided another defence against internal blackness. Heat radiators were fitted all over the theatre to safeguard patrons against chill and a novel system of exhaust piping was installed to draw off smoke from the numerous cigarette and pipe smokers.

Vaudeville, the comprehensive description of the entertainment to be presented by Messrs. Broadhead, twice nightly at 6.50pm and 9.00pm commenced with the matinee performance at 2.30pm on 24th February 1908 of *Grand Vaudeville Entertainment* and competitive to Barrasford's Hippodrome, the popular prices were, orchestra stalls 1/-, grand circle 6d, pit 4d and balcony 3d.

Remaining under the same ownership for 25 years, the Pavilion was among the leading variety theatres in the north of England, after which in May 1933, the entertainment was continued by a new company, the British Theatres Corporation, of which the Chairman was Maurice Voss,

well known in the motor world, whilst Alderman J.C. Cross and Harry Buxton were the joint managing directors of the company which then also controlled the Royal Court Theatre. The Pavilion was closed on 1st July 1933 for a £10,000 scheme of improvements which included external alterations, internal redecorating and re-seating to accommodate a reduced number of 1,700 in luxurious comfort, claimed to outrival that of any other theatre.

In April 1934, the newly appointed chairman was Findley M. Pollack, with Harold Shaw as managing director, Maurice Voss and Alderman Cross having sold their interests and resigned. The continuance of variety entertainment for the further 25 years was interrupted only for a short time during World War II, between October 1940 and 31st March 1941 then reopened with performances at 2.30pm and 6.30pm.

After the war, plans for improvement were approved in December 1946. Two new bars were constructed, waiting room and toilet accommodation was improved, but no alterations were made to the auditorium.

The Pavilion came under new ownership in December 1951, when it was taken over from the British Theatres Corporation for £90,000 by the Manchester based circuit, Brennan's Cinemas Ltd, whose control of the theatre commenced on 31st December 1951, a few days after the start of the Christmas pantomime, *Cinderella* with cast headed by the popular comedian Issy Bonn.

Traditional shows were presented for almost ten more years, by which time the Pavilion had been a variety theatre for over 50 years, and could claim to have featured every top music hall star. But this continuity ended in July 1960 when the company ceased to operate the theatre due to the difficulty in obtaining variety acts, and decreasing admissions as a result of the counter-attraction of television.

The Pavilion was closed for eight months, then leased to a London company, Success Plays Ltd., of which the managing director was the well known comedian and impresario, Terry (Toby Jug) Cantor. Structural alterations were made to the

auditorium appropriate to the new style of future shows and the accent being on glamour, a stage extension was constructed with boardwalk along which the shows girls were to parade into the auditorium above the audience. A £2,000 organ was installed to provide music additional to that of the resident orchestra.

Styled as the New Pavilion Theatre, the great reopening week commenced on 13th March 1961 with *Revue Continental* featuring international star, Jeanne Grozmont, Terry Cantor as the principal comedian, and many artists well known to Merseyside audiences. Advertised as Gay, Gorgeous, Glamourous, the performance in accordance with the new policy was once nightly at 7.15pm. During the half hour prior to the commencement of the show, the audience were entertained by organist Vic Rawlings playing popular melodies on the new theatre organ, then joined with the small orchestra to provide musical accompaniment to the show. A wardrobe of 4,000 costumes was available to the resident company of glamour girls, and a designer was appointed to construct new and different scenes for every production, whilst guest artists were engaged to introduce the acts within the framework of a spectacular revue.

But the venture was short lived for after the summer recess, the performers departed and for the first time bingo sessions were introduced, which although intended by Mr. Cantor as merely a stop gap, soon proved to be the permanent attraction under the ownership of Mecca Ltd., who purchased the theatre from Brennan's Cinemas Ltd., in October 1961 for an undisclosed sum.

Due to the long term popularity of bingo, the Pavilion survived for almost another 25 years until the disastrous fire one night during Easter 1986, when the Edwardian interior and the back stage area were completely destroyed, the only remaining parts of the building being the entrance elevation and the facade. In recent years this has been in use as a venue for snooker and disco, but following the closure of these enterprises in 1992, the entire site was acquired by Gary Armstrong, the pro-

prietor of two bingo halls on Merseyside, the Carlton, Orrell Park, and the Embassy, Seacombe. Mr. Armstrong then instituted the construction of a luxurious 900 seat main hall on the site of the former theatre auditorium and the modernisation and conversion of the old foyer for cash bingo games, using the latest computer technology. Opened on 15th September 1993, the Pavilion Bingo club offers also a fully licensed bar in the main hall and snacks at reasonable prices from the buffet.

1909 WINTER GARDENS THEATRE/APOLLO THEATRE. Pembroke Road, Bootle

Erected in the 1890s the building was originally known as the Beaconsfield Hall used as the Bootle Conservative Club, and later as the County Hall. It was the venue of many big social functions and concerts. In 1909 the hall was acquired by a company, the Suburban Entertainments Syndicate, of which the promoter, Ludwig Blattner stated his intention to convert the hall into a variety theatre to be known as the Winter Gardens, where he would present a high class of entertainment equal to that of any in Liverpool. Extensive alterations and improvements were carried out to adapt the hall for the new purpose and resulted in an auditorium with 490 seats including a small balcony. This was equipped with a cinematograph for the presentation of the latest novelty, animated pictures, as an added attraction to the 'live' entertainment. It was announced that this would be clean, bright and artistic, omitting any feature of vulgarity or bad taste. The seating arrangements were most comfortable, this together with the safety of the public being among the main considerations of the management.

The grand opening under the management of Ludwig Blattner, on 4th May 1909 was attended by a large audience to whom the doors were opened at 7.30pm for the performance at 8.00pm of the Grand High Class Vaudeville Entertainment in which the principal artists were, the old favourite, Billy Richardson, the last of Sam Hague's Minstrels, who provided humour with masterful stump, orations on the topics of the day, Miss Annie Coxon, whose voice was a feature of the programme. Les Curry's clever female artistes in their musical speciality on banjo, concertina and bells and the Sisters Dunville with harmonising contributions. But it was considered that no less important was the contribution to the programme of the renowned Hungarian violin virtuoso, Herr Arnold Spiegler, the musical director and leader of the Bohemian orchestra, for whom the repeated rounds of applause for his skillful playing, reached a climax when the orchestra played a selection from *Tannhauser*. Admission to the orchestra stalls was 1/- and other seats at 6d for this excellent programme which included the latest animated pictures.

During the ensuing two years, control of the Winter Gardens was by three different lessees, the first of these in October 1909, Mr. J. Smith presented variety with the Bohemian orchestra, and Arnold Spiegler was the director of entertainment. After this short regime, the Excelsior Theatre Company in December 1909 opened with variety and animated pictures by the Excelscope, under the management of Mr. George Barry.

On 1st April 1910 it was announced that the theatre was again open to the public under the director of the syndicate, Messrs. Adler, Sutton and Allandale, well known for providing excellent entertainment, by whom the policy of high class variety was continued. Ludwig Blattner resumed his connection with the theatre as joint general manager with Bobbie Allandale, after which, in the August of that year they were co-managing directors. In December 1910 films were presented as the main attraction, advertised as the *Famous Filmograph* supported by high class varieties each evening at 8.00pm to which admission was 1/- to the reserved stalls, 6d and 9d to the balcony.

The next change was to entirely theatrical entertainment by another short term lessee, Mr J.C. Lodge-Percy, who retained the services of Mr. Charles Boult as manager and reopened the Winter Gardens

on 15th April 1911 with Miss Joyce Marsden's high class company in a merry musical farce, *The Girl From Chicago*.

After only two months the theatre was acquired by the New Apollo Syndicate, by whom Ludwig Blattner was appointed as manager, and appropriate to the name of the company the reopening on 19th June 1911 was as the Apollo theatre. The variety of attractions was comprised of The Popular Electric Pictures, including a tale of the wild west, also character and scenic pictures, high class vocalists, and excellent music by England's new violin virtuoso, Mr. E.T. Parcous, who led the orchestra playing selections from *William Tell* and *The Chocolate Soldier* etc.

Coinciding with the coronation of King George V and Queen Mary, the reopening of the theatre was considered to be among the most interesting of the many attractions and entertainments arranged in Bootle. During the following week scenes from the coronation were shown with great clarity to large, enthusiastic audiences.

The reputation of the theatre was further enhanced under the management of Ludwig Blattner, who was later appointed to the position of general manager, but being of German nationality, he was interred an an alien after the outbreak of war in August 1914. But considerably before that time he had severed his connection with the Apollo, which from March of that year had been under new management, the company having appointed John Gaffney as General Manager and Samson Wellings as acting manager, who later became the lessee and manager. In 1916 the Apollo was styled as The Home of Cinema and Music with films accompanied by music of the Apollo orchestra. Performances were nightly at 8.00pm and a children's cinema matinee every Saturday at 3.00pm.

In June 1920, Mr. Wellings made application to the local authorities for permission to construct a new projection room outside the main hall, which in addition to giving a slight increase in the seating accommodation, would serve the greater purpose of better protection for the public in the event of fire, then always a danger with the use of inflammable films.

It transpired however that these improvements were to be enjoyed for a short time only, the last seven months under the control of a syndicate which included Harry and Stanley Pennington, whose family were well known in the district for their establishment of the Royal Muncaster and Metropole theatres. The Apollo was taken over from Samson Wellings in December 1922, when it was announced that the entertainment policy would continue as previously. But this proved to be for a short time only for the Apollo finally closed as a cinema on 22nd July 1923. The feature film was the western drama starring William Russell, *The Strength of the Pines* with the supporting programme of *Fireside Brew-*

ers, Eve's Review, pictorial and graphic.

Structural alterations were carried out during the following two months, after which the building reverted back to its former use and name, the County Hall. Opening in October 1923, it was stated to be the finest and most up to date hall in the district, available for receptions etc. and dances in the large ballroom.

The chequered history of the hall came to an abrupt end in 1941 when it was severely damaged during an air raid, and stood partly demolished until 1948 when the site was cleared. For many years this has been occupied by the playground of St. Winifred's girls school near to the Bootle, Oriel Road railway station.

1909 THE BIJOU THEATRE/BIJOU ELECTRIC PALACE/ BIJOU CINEMA, East Street, Waterloo

Erected in 1840, the building was the birthplace of many religious societies, and churches of different denominations were established within its walls. About the turn of the century it was a Salvation Army Citadel, then a Presbyterian Mission. Later known as the East Street Assembly Rooms it was a venue for concerts, re-unions and various functions until the opening of newer halls offering better facilities.

The building began a really new lease of life in 1909 when the then dingy hall was acquired by the enterprising lessees and managers, Messrs Weber, Son & Arnold who instituted the conversion into a bright and cosy little theatre. Professor Weber, as he was known, was a well known artiste who not only entertained, but mystified his audience. Arthur Weber was famous for his magnificent voice and musical skill, by which he had gained a reputation, not only on local concert platforms, but in larger towns.

The opening of the districts first permanent venue of live entertainment was a significant event in the quiet suburb and it was reported that in the improved and newly

decorated interior, the once dingy Assembly Rooms could hardly be recognised. Re-seating was to a capacity of about 300, of which the red plush tip-up seats at the front were separated from those at the rear by a wooden partition.

The public extended a generous patronage on the Saturday evening of 5th June 1909 and showed their appreciation of the miscellaneous items of the variety performance which commenced at 8.00pm. This included lessees Professor Weber with ventriloquial entertainment and Arthur Weber as the principal singer. Music was by the orchestra under the direction of Monsieur Ernest Wilinski and the performance was concluded by animated pictures on the cinematograph illustrating *Coney Island at Night, A Convict's Escape* and *A Sound Sleeper* for which prices of admission were 1/-, 6d and 3d.

During the following year the theatre was known as the New Pavilion, then the Palace Music Hall during the brief term as lessees of the Empire Enterprise Company, but the name Bijou was restored c1912 by lessee and manager William Eltoft, by whom it was run as a cinema, the Bijou Electric Palace and later, the Bijou Cinema until towards the end of 1918, when Mr Eltoft was forced to relinquish his position due to bad health.

He was succeeded by the cinema's last lessee, Walter Jackson, who on 8th January 1919 gave a special benefit performance for Mr Eltoft at which he presented the former lessee with a handsome gold watch amidst cheers from the audience, who packed the hall to capacity.

The Bijou survived four more years against strong competition from the district's first purpose-built cinema, the Queen's in South Road, and finally closed in November 1922. The building was later used by a private hire firm, Brady's Taxi Cabs, then for many years as a motor cycle repair depot until the late 1980s when it was demolished and the site redeveloped with residential property.

1911 METROPOLE THEATRE, Stanley Road, Bootle

At the time 20 years after the opening of the Royal Muncaster Theatre, Irlam Road, by the Pennington Estate Co. Ltd. there was a widely held opinion among residents that the district was lacking in public amusements, and that there was a need for a really first class theatre. Although the Muncaster was considered most comfortable and presenting fine performances, its situation had considerably deteriorated due to the nearby warehouses and timber yards. Messrs. Pennington therefore decided in 1910 on the building of the handsome and palatial theatre to be known as the Metropole, in a central main road position on the tram car route, and within five minutes walk of the Marsh Lane station on the Lancashire & Yorkshire railway.

Designed in the Renaissance style by Messrs. Havelock Sutton & Sons, the well known theatre architects of Dale Street, Liverpool, the building had an ornate five storey facade, 80ft in width. The construction was of brick and stone the latter being used to form an attractive setting for the numerous windows, the central balcony at second floor level and the panel above bearing the theatre name. Across almost the entire frontage extended an ornamental verandah of iron and wire woven glass with lead-light glazing, and metal centre-piece with holders for the torch-style shaded electric lamps. The upper part of the frontage being illuminated by shaded lamps suspended from metal brackets.

The central main entrance was in the form of two wide arches, each with two pairs of elaborate mahogany doors, which gave access to the entrance hall with mosaic flooring and tiled dado. From this area, two wide staircases conducted patrons to the mezzanine floor above, which contained the circle refreshment buffet, the gentlemen's cloakrooms and staircases descending to the stalls. At a higher level, entrance to the dress circle was by two wide folding doors in the well furnished lounge, which also included the ladies' cloakrooms.

The most remarkable feature of the auditorium, which had seating accommodation for 1,850 people, including the boxes, each with 12 seats, at either side of the auditorium was that by the cleverness of the planning, the circles were unusually close to the stage. It was expected therefore, that patrons of those parts of the house would appreciate this sense of contiguity, both from the point of view of hearing as well as seeing the performance. It was reported that the Metropole was the first theatre in England to be built on this principle, and due to the fact that the stalls seats were not fitted directly behind those of the row in front, it was justifiably claimed that a clear view of the stage could be obtained from practically every seat in the areas designated as boxes, stalls, pit stalls, dress circle, upper circle and gallery.

The decorative treatment was artistic throughout and with prevailing colours of white and crimson stood out in bold relief. The ceiling, the proscenium and the circle fronts were adorned by finely modeled fibrous plaster work in heavy relief, and finished in white and against the rich crimson on the walls, the velvet coverings of the seats and carpets of the same colour, a pleasant contrast was provided, giving a touch of warmth and comfort to the auditorium.

The proscenium opening was 36ft by 30ft. The stage 75ft in width and 27ft deep and sufficiently large to enable Mr. Harry Pennington to present the most elaborate of productions.

A great deal of interest was evident in the opening of this new enterprise of the Pennington Estate Company. On Monday, 20th February 1911, attended by the Mayor and Mayoress of Bootle, Councillor and Mrs. J.R. Barbour, and several hundred guests at the invitation of the company, it was an occasion of prime importance. Stanley Road was illuminated by the brilliant arc lamps on the tall facade adorned by festoons of flags, as a great crowd of people congregated outside to witness the arrival of the Mayor and Mayoress.

In the theatre, the large audience was entertained with musical selections by the orchestra conducted by Mr. Tom Shaw until everything was ready for the opening ceremony, which began with the managing director, Harry Pennington stepping in front of the footlights, and before the elegant new act drop with painted view of the Grand Canal, Venice, to a great outburst of enthusiastic applause.

Then followed speeches by Mr. Pennington and the Mayor, who declared the theatre open, touching the button of a 'live' electric cable by which the drop scene ascended to reveal the spacious stage, brightened with new and artistic equipment, and illuminated by a carefully arranged system of lighting. Following this the *National Anthem* was sung, the audience joined in, and after a short interval, the opening attraction was Mr. Andie Caine's company's production of the pantomime *Little Red Riding Hood*. This was chosen by Mr. Pennington with the object of striking a popular note for

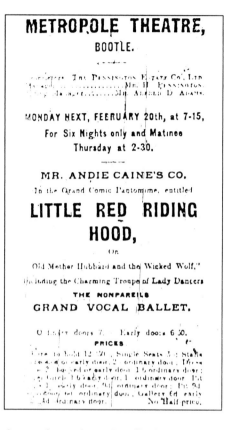

the opening and was described as a particularly light and vivacious entertainment full of melody, mirth and mimicry in nine elaborate scenes. A special feature of the admission prices was that the boxes seating 12 could be booked for 30/-, the charge for a single seat being 3/-. Admission to the orchestra stalls was 2/6d, and at descending cost, dress circle 2/-, upper circle 1/6d, pit 9d, gallery 4d, and 6d.

The theatre enjoyed remarkable success from the time of opening and after pantomime there was a quick change to Shakespearian plays the following week. During the years until the early twenties, the Metropole was established as a legitimate theatre presenting comic and dramatic plays, also musical comedies with a once nightly policy.

The prosperity and popularity of the theatre was increasing, when in 1922 Harry Pennington, then a Councillor and a J.P. found that the increase of his public and social activities and the strain of business were becoming a serious tax upon his time and strength. It was subsequently announced that the theatre had been acquired by a small

syndicate of local gentlemen, headed by Arthur Smith, proprietor of the *Bootle Times* as Chairman, and in the position of managing director, J. Leslie Greene, former lessee of the Sun Hall cinema, who in addition to being Chairman of the Liverpool Branch, Cinematograph Exhibitors Association, was also a director of the Southport Palladium, the Hope Hall cinema, Liverpool, and the Kingsway cinema, Hoylake. The final week of the old regime ended on Saturday, 25th March 1922 with the Rennef American company of actors, vocalists and dancers

presentation of *Uncle Tom's Cabin*, a musical play based on Harriet Beecher Stowe's famous book.

The new company named the Bootle Metropole Syndicate spent several thousand pounds on improvements, of which about £2,000 was on the new stalls seats of dark mahogany with bronze standards and upholstery covering of old rose plush. The orchestra stalls were completed with a rich dark blue Wilton carpet and other parts by cork linoleum, whilst screens of dark stained woodwork were built around the sides and

the rear of the stalls to prevent draught. Another great improvement was that it would not in future be necessary for patrons of the stalls to ascend the stairs, stalls entrances having been created in the main entrance hall, the floor of which was in a neat design of cream and green tiling harmonising with the dado. The walls of the auditorium, also the gallery and circle fronts were thoroughly renovated, whilst the dado around the stalls was painted a rich brown, appropriate to the old rose colour of the seats and dark stain of the woodwork. The ceilings of the soffit of the circles were painted in cream, whilst the whole of the main ceiling and gold paintwork were renovated and re-burnished. Curtains of rich old rose velour enhanced the whole effect to give a rich oriental effect of great beauty and charm.

The aim of the company was that the Metropole should continue to be a first class house of entertainment, providing at popular prices, plays, operas, musical comedies and other productions by number one companies. In accordance with this policy the opening attraction on Easter Monday, 17th April 1922 was the famous musical comedy *To-Night's The Night* presented by George G. Sharpe's Company, as played at the Gaiety Theatre, London for over two years.

The Metropole presented mainly twice nightly revue and vaudeville entertainment during the 1920's and until 1931, then facing strong competition from sound films, showing at many cinemas in the district. The company closed the theatre on 27th June 1931 for extensive internal alterations for a new entertainment policy of cine-variety.

An entirely new upper circle was constructed and fitted with tip-up seats,

which also replaced the benches in the gallery, where the seating capacity was reduced by 400 to provide space in the centre for the projection room, in which was installed Western Electric sound system. As at other theatres coverted for showing films from the highest floor level, this was achieved only by a very steep angle of projection to a rather small squarish screen, angled back accordingly on the stage.

For the grand reopening on August bank holiday, Monday 3rd August 1931, the Metropole presented the first of the new programmes of Star Pictures and Star Variety, with a matinee at 2.30pm and a continuous performance from 6.30pm. On the screen *The Lottery Bride* starred the famous American actress and singer, Jeanette MacDonald and on the stage was the latest continental entertainment *La Grande Revuette at Cie*. This continued throughout the week, but the film was changed on Thursday to *Framed*, featuring Evelyn Brent, and the film programmes included British Movietone News. The admission prices of 6d to 1/3d were reduced to 4d, 6d, and 8d at the matinees.

Continuing under the control of the

same company, but known as the Metropole Theatre (Bootle) Ltd., performances of cine-variety were presented until April 1934, then reverting back to revues and variety shows. But the shortage of variety acts in the early war years resulted in a return of cine-variety on 7th October 1940 with the film *Keep Your Seats Please* starring George Formby, also a star variety bill and quick fire talent finding contest. But this type of entertainment proved to be short lived, for on 23rd November 1940 the Metropole was closed until further notice.

The Grand Gala reopening took place on Monday, 5th May 1941 with Rations Unlimited at 6.30 and 8.30pm with full variety company and to celebrate the occasion, Monday night was Gift Night when 10/- notes were given away! But this proved to be the shortest of opening periods, for this was the last week of nightly German air raids on Merseyside, known as the May Blitz, and during one of these on 7th May the theatre was destroyed.

The site was subsequently cleared, but for many years was occupied only by two large advertisement hoardings, until redeveloped in the early 1980s with the present restaurant and amusement arcade.

1913
CRANE HALL/CRANE THEATRE/
NEPTUNE THEATRE.
Hanover Street

Of all Liverpool's theatres, that which since 1968 has been known as the Neptune may surely claim the distinction of the most unusual location, being sited high on the upper floors of the tall Crane building, with access from the corner main entrance by a long spiral staircase.

The Crane Hall, as it was originally named, was built in 1913 by the Crane Brothers, musical instrument and music dealers, who moved from their Scotland Road premises to Hanover Street, where it was one of the largest music stores in the north. Above the store was constructed a concert hall with a platform on the right of the present rear stalls entrances, however, one of the Crane sons, being a member of the Green Room considered that a theatre would have more uses than a concert hall. The company then purchased an adjacent 130 year old building for the construction of the present stage, with the fly tower sited in a Mansard roof. This is a roof with a top much flatter than normal, but before reaching the line at the outer walls it slopes steeply to meet them, so forming a space in which rooms can be constructed. Although then fully equipped as a theatre, the name Crane Hall was retained until 1938 when it became known as the Crane Theatre.

With a seating capacity of 451 it was considered of comfortable size without being too overpowering for the amateur actor and ideally situated in the city centre, it became the home of amateur drama, although professional companies have always been encouraged to use the theatre, and have frequently done so.

Despite the continued use by Merseyside drama groups and the appearance of well known actors, actresses and musicians, the theatre was threatened with closure in 1966. This caused great alarm in amateur dramatic circles, but following a period of great uncertainty about its future,

the Liverpool Corporation took a 21 year lease on the premises in August 1967 thereby assuring the amateur companies of a permanent home.

During the summer closure in 1968 work proceeded on rejuvenating the theatre at a cost of nearly £7,000. The interior was completely transformed, being repainted and recarpeted, new curtains were installed, and the 451 seats were dismantled in twelve hours by sixty volunteers and sent to London for recovering. Appropriate to the latest theatrical style, an 8ft apron stage was constructed with two extra entrances from left and right immediately on to the apron, which was removable to make room for the orchestra pit. The old footlights were removed, lighting of the stage then being from numerous spotlights mounted around the 26ft by 13ft proscenium, whilst above the stage were 25 flying lines for the drop scenes. The bar was rearranged to allow at least two walls to be used as an art gallery and modernised to serve also as a buffet with attractive modern decor and design, whilst a new lift from street level to the foyer was installed.

The alterations were all supervised by the new theatre manager, appointed by the Corporation, Teresa Collard, formerly a London theatre administrator who had studied at the Royal Academy of Dramatic Art.

Since the theatre was no longer associated with the Crane Brothers, and to complete the transformation, it was given its present name, the Neptune, appropriate to the figure which forms part of the city's Coat of Arms.

The extensive programme drawn up for the Autumn season by Teresa Collard commenced on the evening of 26th September 1968 when the theatre was officially opened with Henrick Ibsen's *An Enemy of the People* performed by a cast of players drawn from the leading amateur dramatic societies in the city, and was directed by Teresa Collard.

During that season fifteen companies staged productions such as *The Anniversary, Its Never Too Late* and *La Gioconda,* also professional productions included the special Christmas show *Beauty and the Beast* and the *Gilbert and Sullivan for All Company.*

The second stage of re-furbishment in 1969 was mainly concerned with the back stage and main staircase areas, but there was also rewiring throughout and the installation of a mechanical lifting device for the safety curtain. In the summer of

1970, six balcony seats were removed for the installation of the first fully electronic lighting switchboard in a Liverpool theatre, also a control room for a new sound system.

The following is a brief description of the theatre, which remains little changed since its re-opening in 1968.

The long and wide spiral staircase with polished wood dado and balustrade leads up to a rectangular foyer with booking office, refreshment kiosk, and access on the right to the licensed bar. In the centre two pairs of doors lead into the enclosed central portion of the rear stalls crossover gangway of the practically square-shaped auditorium. Although most of the seating is in the three sections across the stalls floor, there is also a shallow balcony which does not overhang the lower floor and is reached from the foyer entrance by a continuation of the spiral staircase.

The auditorium is notable for the extensive use of polished mahogany, which forms an attractive dado around the walls, whilst above, large panels and the carved cornice are picked out in white against a base colour of dark green. The straight ceiling is similarly decorated and provides the principal illumination with a central chandelier of globe- shaded lights and others of a similar type fitted flush to the ceiling. Spaced around the walls are elegant brass light fittings with torch style shades, and the carved heads of famous composers.

Formed in 1969, the Neptune Theatre Company gained a loyal following, and a very good reputation, performing three or more three act plays each year, and a Christmas play for children, commencing with *Toad of Toad Hall*. Children were also remembered throughout the year with companies such as Polka Children's Theatre and Playboard Puppets presenting shows for children of all ages.

The original brief from the Liverpool Corporation was therefore fulfilled, in that the theatre should be used for professional, amateur and children's theatre, and to encourage the standards of amateur productions.

In 1973 Teresa Collard was succeeded as theatre manager by Sylvia Wooldridge, who had come to the Neptune as a clerical assistant in 1968, and for 20 years prior to her recent retirement had been in overall charge of the theatre's affairs from finance and licensing to planning the year's programmes.

For many years the reputation of the Neptune has continued to rest principally on the repertory company, but it remains well known for children's productions, especially the sell out Christmas shows. It is also the annual March venue for the Gilbert and Sullivan Amateur Operatic Society, and the only home in the city for amateur theatre groups and dance schools.

In recent times the theatre has been used increasingly by professional touring companies, by one of which the staging for 10 weeks during 1992 of the Dublin play *Goodbye to the Hill* was a record run. Many well known actors have appeared at the Neptune including Dame Judi Dench, actor husband Michael Williams, the late Kenneth Moore and Irish actor and raconteur, Michael Macliarmoir, as well as a host of past and present stars of television's *Brookside*.

To all those interested in the various aspects of theatre at the Neptune the threat of closure announced in the spring of 1993, came not only as a surprise but a severe blow to the groups, which could not, due to financial restraints, transfer to other venues.

This arose from an adverse report on the theatre commissioned by the council and Liverpool City challenge, which recommended that the council, by whom performances were funded with a grant of £119,000 in the current year should relinquish their lease with the owners, Crane's Music Store. The criticism was refuted by the council's arts working party, which pledged its support for the theatre, stating that it was vital to Liverpool. A campaign to save it was backed by Dame Judi Dench and Michael Williams, which was fortunately successful, and as a result of this, the Neptune remains as Liverpool's only Civic Theatre, described by the Theatre's Trust as one of the 50 most architecturally significant theatres in the country. It is a listed building with an auditorium as it was in 1913, and in 1993 celebrated its 80th birthday and its silver jubilee of council owner-ship.

Although essentially a civic theatre, it now boasts an ever increasing programme of professional shows providing a desirable mix of amateurs and professionals, but whilst the latter give the theatre a higher profile, it is the former which keeps the Neptune viable.

At this time in the mid 1990s, a bright future is indicated for the theatre, which is attracting wider audiences than ever in previous years.

1915 EMPIRE THEATRE, James Street, Garston

As a theatre of 'live' entertainment, the Empire has the distinction of being Liverpool's shortest surviving, having been in this use only from June 1915 until September 1918. This began a period of 44 years as a cinema, followed by about 30 years to date as a bingo and social club.

The first scheme for the new Empire theatre originated in November 1912, when the Garston Empire and Picture Theatre Company submitted their application with plans by architect Cecil Massey of London, to the Chairman of the council, for a theatre seating 1,050 in the stalls and 436 in the circle. It was to have a full sized stage with 'fly' facilities, eight dressing rooms and a Biograph box, equipped with a cinematograph. The application having been refused, a successful application was made in January 1913 by Thomas, George Carroll of Granby Street, Liverpool, but his scheme was abandoned, as also a further proposed venture in July 1913 of the Garston Empire and Picture Theatre Co., whose plans were used for the subsequent building.

Having already approved two schemes to no avail, the council were not at first favourable to another application on 2nd April 1914 by Alfred Wright, a produce broker of Sefton Park, but since this was for a picture hall with two already operating in the district, the Garston Picturedrome, Heald

Street and the Lecture Hall, Wellington Street, the application was adjourned for three months, after which Mr. Wright was required to prove the need for another. The plans were later approved and the date of notice for permission to build was 30th July 1914.

The building was erected at a cost of £7,500 including the site by the Liverpool contractors, R. Costain & Son, with plans which differed from those of the original only by the addition of two stage boxes, and a reduction in the seating capacity to 1,040 of which 336 were in the circle.

On the site at the junction of James Street and Church Road, the construction was almost entirely of ordinary brick, with the exception of the left side of the James Street frontage of red brick, which was also used to form an arch above the first and second floor windows. The upper part of the three storey frontage was recessed from right to left, the ground floor part of the elevation including the main entrance projecting forward adjacent to the road. The main entrance gave access to a rectangular foyer with a short flight of marble steps opposite, which led into a waiting room with three entrance to the rear of the stalls. At the extreme left of the foyer, an enclosed marble staircase with metal balustrade was ascended to the first floor lounge, beyond which a staircase led to the back circle entrance. The seating was arranged in two blocks with centre and side gangways on a stepped floor which descended to the curved front terminating at the box on either side of the proscenium. The circle front was ornamented with plasterwork panels, and brackets suspending shaded electric lamps were spaced around. The boxes with half circular fronts, also richly ornamented by plaster work, were flanked by substantial marble columns with carved capitals at either side of the high, arched proscenium of approximately 30ft width. The auditorium was illuminated principally by glass-shaded electric lamps in large fittings suspended from the carved ribs spaced along the curved ceiling.

Full theatrical facilities including an orchestra pit were included, appropriate to the fact that the first licence granted on 1st

June 1915 was for Theatre, Music Hall and Cinematograph. The first official notice of the opening was in the trade press *Kinematograph Weekly* of 10th June 1915 in which it was reported that the Empire had opened on the afternoon of Saturday, 5th June under the management of Mr. Charles Locke, when a large crowd was present. The first advertisement in the local press appeared on Monday, 14th June for Comedy-Variety-Pictures, twice nightly at 6.45pm and 9.00pm, admission prices, stalls 6d, circle 9d and 1/-.

Mr. Locke's policy of variety and pictures remained until 1916, when it was announced that from 3rd April, stage plays only were to be presented. Then in 1917 there was another change to variety shows and revues until the Empire ended its short life as a theatre on 31st August 1918 with variety entertainment entitled *Mr. & Mrs. John Bull at Home*.

The Empire began its 44 years' life as a cinema on 2nd September 1918 with the Star Exclusive Picture Attraction, *The Heart Of A Lion*, also supporting programme including the latest *Topical Gazette* and musical accompaniment by the Empire augmented orchestra.

In July 1928 the theatre was taken over from the proprietors, Garston Theatre and Empire Pictures Ltd., by the J.F. Woods cinema circuit, from that time known as Bedford Cinemas (1928) Ltd.

Sound films commenced on 16th June 1930 with *The Gold Diggers of Broadway* the theatre having been equipped with Western Electric sound system, after which it was run by the same proprietors until 8th December 1962 when the final film programme was the double feature, *Jailhouse Rock*, starring Elvis Presley also *The Fastest Gun Alive*.

Although the Empire went over to full time bingo on 10th December 1962, this was first introduced in August of that year on Sundays only, then increased to three evenings weekly in October.

A new trading company, Empire Bingo and Social Club (Garston) Ltd., was then formed with directorate including Mr. R.I. Godfrey, managing director of Cheshire County Cinemas, but Bedford Cinemas continued to hold an interest in the enterprise until 1986, when this was acquired by Mr. Andrew Sale of J. & A. Entertainments, Kirby, who then became the sole proprietor of the Empire.

Since that time there has been considerable re-furbishment and redecoration. The former cinema seats on the ground floor were replaced by red covered, comfortably upholstered, bench type seats around tables, whilst below the stage, a licensed bar was constructed with access by a stairway in the centre of the front crossover gangway,

It is interesting to observe that despite the changes of use since the opening in 1915 the auditorium retains many of the original architectural features. The boxes have suitable drapes and crystal chandeliers, whilst the fibrous plaster designs of the fronts, as those of the circle and proscenium are appropriately picked out against the general decorative scheme of a principally warm colour.

The Empire remains among the theatres and cinemas throughout the country which continue to exist due to the attraction of bingo.

**1922
WINTER GARDENS
THEATRE,
Church Road, Waterloo**

Records indicate that the building was probably erected in the 1870s and that it was a large gymnasium in 1890 when it was owned by Alfred T. Davies, Lloyd George's political agent. Later a billiard hall, other kinds of entertainment were held until conversion to a cinema, the New

Picture Hall in 1909. It was first known as the Winter Gardens in February 1910 and from April 1914 as the Waterloo Picture Playhouse until closing on 29th July 1922 when the silent feature film was entitled *The Carnival of Truth* and supporting programme included the serial *The Lurking Devil*.

The hall was then acquired by a company of which the managing director was the enterprising Frederick V. Ross, then a well known figure in the sphere of variety entertainment, who for seven years until September 1921 had successfully run the Tivoli, New Brighton with this type of entertainment.

To the plans of architect Colin S. Brothers of Liverpool, the place was practically rebuilt by the contractors, Messrs J.M. Milestone & Son Ltd who it was stated, carried out the plans with great accuracy and admirable finish. The new design of the exterior was considered striking with ornamental gables and picturesque outline. The new main frontage to Church Road and the rear adjacent to Olive Road were faced with matt white stone without ornamentation, and relieved only by numerous small windows. This was on three levels, at the left the three storey elevation included the stage block with stage door, surmounted by a large electric sign with the new name, Winter Gardens. Between this and the two storey elevation at the opposite end, a single storey splayed section was constructed for the main entrance. A glass canopy extended along this and the side elevation to Olive Road.

Extensive internal alterations increased the seating capacity from 450 to about 650 by the construction of an entirely new straight fronted balcony with accommodation for 170 patrons with new entrances and exits. In the stalls the seating was increased to about 480 by increasing the width of the lower floor for the side gangways, the upper part of the walls being supported by plain columns. To ensure that patrons would enjoy the performance in perfect comfort, tip-up seats were fitted in every part of the house and a complete new heating and ventilating scheme was adopted. The plain style of decorations was described as on the futuristic principle.

On the occasion of the reopening on 25th September 1922 the hall became again the Winter Gardens from its early cinema days, but then in its new role as a theatre. A large crowd assembled outside, but many went away disappointed, unable to gain admission as the auditorium was filled to capacity in a very short time. Alderman T.S. Ashmole of Wallasey during a short speech from the stage congratulated the builders and architect upon the wonderful transformation of the building which had been made in only seven weeks. He also congratulated Frederick Ross, whose name was a household word, in connection with the live entertainment upon his new venture and hoped that residents of the district would show their appreciation of the high class entertainments to be provided by patronising the Winter Gardens. In future this was to be confined solely to vaudeville, musical and straight plays, but films would

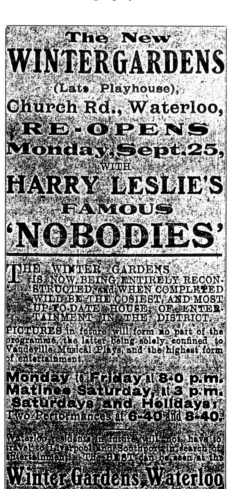

form no part of the programme.

Appropriately the new theatre was inaugurated by a performance of variety entertainment at 8.00pm entitled *Harry Leslie's Famous Nobodies*. Future performances were to be at 8.00pm from Monday to Friday, a matinee on Saturdays at 3.00pm, and twice nightly on Saturdays and bank holidays at 6.40pm and 8.40pm. Admission was at 9d, 1/3d and 1/10d

This began the Winter Gardens nine years of life as a theatre, during which a great range of entertainment was presented, for apart from revues and variety, during the late twenties and into the 1930s, many comedy and dramatic plays were produced, noteable among which were those of Edward Banstan's talented repertory company, whose attractions during two seasons in 1930 varied from Shakespeare's *The Taming of the Shrew* and *King Lear* to the drama *Interference* and the hilarious *Hawleys of the High Street*.

A variety show *The First Army Follies* ended on 28th June 1930 and the theatre was then closed until 4th August, then reopened with Road Show of 1930 advertised as everything that is best in vaudeville performed by sixteen artists. The year ended with a return visit of Sydney Monckton, Esme Lewis and full London company in the West End farces *Rookery Nook* and *Love at Second Sight* after which, in January 1931, the last theatrical manager, Max Wakeman instituted a twice nightly entertainment season and reduced prices of admission, continuing the previous entertainment policy but the final closure as a theatre on 27th June 1931 was at the end of a week of nightly changed productions by the Godwin Opera Company.

It was then announced that the Winter Gardens was to be closed for extensive redecoration and reconditioning for the reversion to a cinema, catching up with the latest craze, the "talkies", equipped with BTP sound system. The reopening took place on 26th December 1931 with the feature film *Lets Live and Laugh* featuring Ronald Frankau, an appropriate choice since the British artist had appeared in 1930 on the Winter Garden's stage in his variety show *Cabaret Kittens*. The supporting programme consisted of comedy, interest and the news-reel to which the popular prices of admission were 7d, 9d, and 1/3d at the two separate evening performances, 6.30pm and 8.40pm, the opening being on a Saturday. Monday to Friday these were to be continuous from 6.30pm and matinees on Monday, Wednesday and Saturday at 3.00pm.

The Winter Gardens was then under the management of Mr. Horace C. Lewis, who had been connected with the film business for some years, having occupied the position of managing director and chairman of the Alhambra Cinema, London Road, Liverpool (then closed to reopen as the King's in 1932). Mr. Lewis therefore had experience of the exhibition and renting of films, and in a position to book the best available.

The use as a cinema was continued by the Winter Gardens Talkie Theatre (1933) Ltd., under the management of Mr. A.J. Willett and for 20 years from 1945 by the Heyes family, under whose control it survived to become the last privately owned cinema in north Merseyside. Although a cinema for over 30 years, the stage was regularly used, this being the venue for the productions of the Waterloo and Crosby Amateur Operatic Society. These terminated in the early 1960s when the stalls seating was removed to accommodate another attraction after an experiment with bingo sessions had failed, beat dances for teenagers on Saturday and Sunday evenings.

With a film booking policy including a large proportion of 'X' certificate films, changed three or four times weekly, and the introduction of other attractions, the Winter Gardens survived for many years after larger cinemas had closed, but finally, rising costs, dwindling audiences and stiff competition forced the booking manager and joint director, Mr. Henry Derek Heyes to close the theatre, after nearly 56 years as a place of entertainment. The final performance was the afternoon matinee on 4th September 1965 with the feature film *The Train* featuring Burt Lancaster.

Although the building had been offered to the local authorities, it lay unused until 1982, when it was acquired by a religious order, the Kingsway Christian Fellowship. The entire frontage was then demolished and replaced by the present one of red brick with the entrance way projecting forward at the extreme left, leaving only the greatly altered former auditorium and the roof.

The building was opened as a new church centre in April 1983.

1925 EMPIRE THEATRE, Lime Street

The present Empire Theatre was constructed on the site of the former theatre of the same name, previously known as the Alexandra. The new theatre was shown for the first time in all its white, gold and scarlet glory on 3rd March 1925 to selected guests including the Liverpool City Engineer, Mr. J. Brodie, who stated that it was among the finest constructed theatres he had seen.

Mr. R.H. Gillespie, managing director of the proprietors, Moss Empires Ltd., informed those present that the company had opted for a theatre which would not only be worthy of the site, but one which would incorporate every feature and improvement in theatre construction. With this aim in view, Mr. Gillespie, accompanied by Mr. T.R. Milburn the architect, had made a special journey to the United States to study theatre construction, before undertaking the Liverpool venture. The result was considered unique for it was not a copy of any other theatre, although including ideas and principles common to the best theatres in England, Wales and the U.S.A.

The wide and imposing facade constructed of Portland stone differed only to a small extent from its present appearance, originally there were three main entrance ways in the centre, and a wide exit way at the extreme right, later replaced by an advertising display window, whilst the canopy facia displayed the theatre name and that of the proprietors.

The constructors of the building and the company responsible for the contracting out of the specialist work were Messrs. W.M. Moss and Sons Ltd., of London and Liverpool, who had completed, or had in course of construction, some of Liverpool's finest buildings.

The *Liverpool Daily Courier* reported that the first impression on entering the auditorium was a sense of spaciousness, the stalls floor having 1,350 seats, whilst above the circle with front curving to the long splayed walls at either side of the proscenium, provided seating for 1,100 people, all free from pillars or posts to

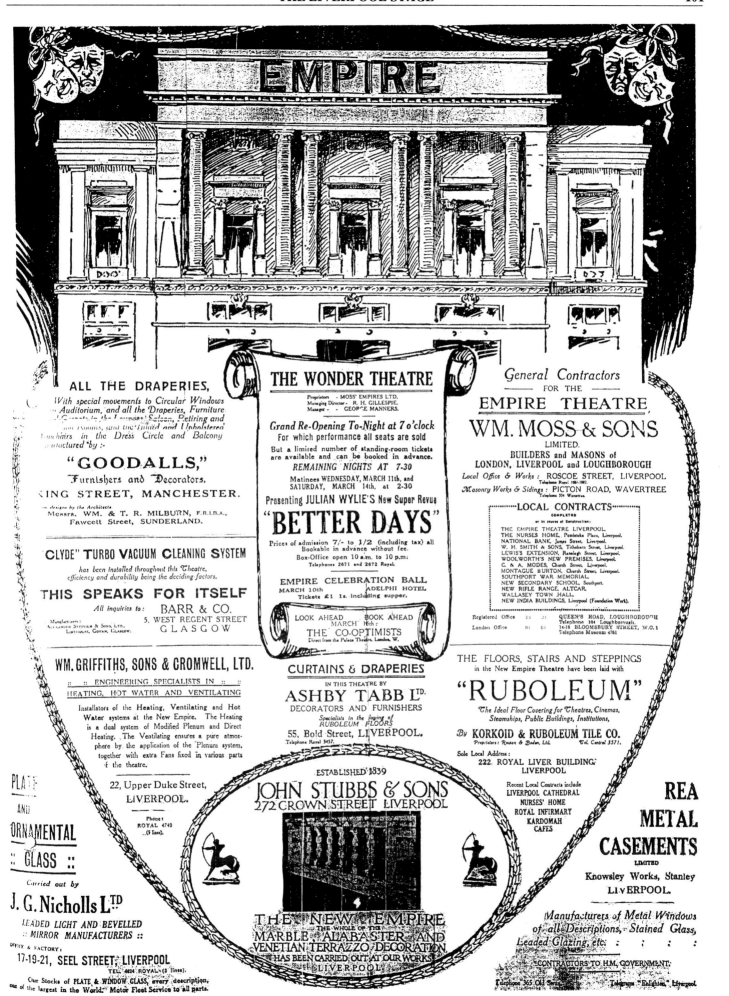

impair the sight lines, and about half the stalls floor was stepped.

The Empire was stated to have the largest stage in Great Britain, being 160ft in width and 40ft deep. The proscenium arch, about 60ft wide was set within a massive curved area, decorated by panels, which curved from the ceiling terminated above the stage box at either side. These originally projected over the front of the stalls to provide a view of the stage from the line of seats adjacent to the box front. With this exception practically all the architectural features remain, among which possibly the most impressive is the large, oval ceiling dome over the front part of the circle. In the centre of this was originally suspended a chandelier with changing coloured lights,

and a further 200 concealed in a recess around the outer edge of the dome. A remarkable system of concealed lighting was also fitted behind classic urns abutting the ceiling, all providing a soft light evenly diffused over the whole auditorium. Above the ground floor, a golden glow was distributed from numerous shaded light fittings on the soffit of the balcony, whilst on the front were mounted spotlights of 1,000 candle power for stage lighting.

A notable feature of the interior was the great amount of marble which was used, not only for every staircase and in the waiting areas, but also in the auditorium for attractive balustrades. The orchestra pit provided space for thirty musicians, but for operatic performances a platform could be

placed flush with the auditorium floor to accommodate additional players. Backstage the comfort of the artists received special consideration, a lift being provided to take them up to the dressing rooms at various floor levels, stated to be the first with showers ever seen in a British theatre.

Although spacious refreshment salons had been provided and placed conveniently at the rear of the auditorium, a surprising omission from the original plans was a licensed bar! Apparently the reason was that the Empire had to some extent been modelled on the style of a New York Theatre, built at the time of prohibition. Bars were added later, one in the basement reached by stairways from the rear stalls and the other, for circle patrons, in the first floor lounge.

Rebuilt and enlarged to its present size, then stated to be larger than the London Palladium and the most up-to-date theatre in the provinces, the Empire Theatre opened on 9th March 1925 with the new style super revue by Julian Wylie, *Better Days*, starring Stanley Lupino, Maisie Gay and Ruth

French. This opening production was for the first time on any stage and prior to its presentation at the London Hippodrome. Seats for the performance at 7.00pm were at prices from 1/2d to 7/-, but only a limited number of standing room tickets were available, the seats having been fully booked

weeks in advance, with thousands of hopefuls all over the country having their cheques and postal orders returned.

Those fortunate to have tickets were overjoyed with the new theatre which caused

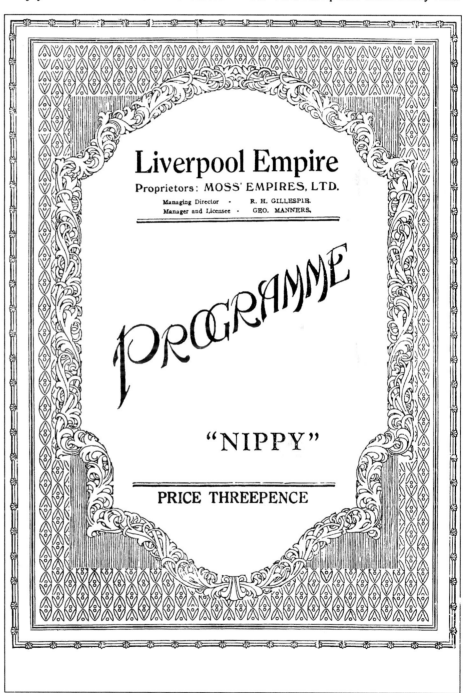

such a sensation that, according to one report, an admirer lost his glass eye!

Following the opening attraction, the 1920s were noteable for big musical

productions, once nightly, which included C.B. Cochran's *On with the Dance*, and prior to London presentations in 1926, *Lady be Good* with cast headed by Fred and Adele Astaire and *The Apache* with Dorothy Ward

and Shaun Glenville. Also in the cast was Carl Brisson, later to become famous as a Hollywood star of film musicals in the 1930s. There was also *No, No, Nannete* and the

Drury Lane production of *Rose Marie,* but a contrast was provided by such attractions as *St Joan* with Sybil Thorndike and visits of the British National Opera Co. presenting nightly changes of well known operas.

In 1930 the famous actress Tallulah Bankhead, after seven years stage experience made two of her last stage appearances at the Empire in *The Lady of the Camelias* on 2nd June and in *Let Us be Gay* on 11th August before departing for Hollywood in 1931 to begin a new career as a film actress with Paramount Pictures in *Tarnished Lady.* The fact that talking pictures were then providing considerable opposition to the live theatre apparently prompted the production of Francis Laidler's revue, *The Reply to the Talkies,* which was the August Bank Holiday attraction on 4th August 1930.

Up to about the mid 1930s the Empire presented a great many musicals such as *Maid of the Mountains, The Desert Song, Rio Rita, The Merry Widow* and *White Horse Inn,* but during the latter half of the decade the concentration was more on twice nightly variety shows, some featuring famous bands such as those of Henry Hall, Jack Hylton and Harry Roy, whilst others had as top of the bill attraction, artists such as Gracie Fields, Lupino Lane, Elsie and Doris Waters and Arthur Tracy, the "Street Singer".

Remaining open during the war years, variety performances continued with many favourites of that time, Liverpool comedians, Arthur Askey and Rob Wilton, also Tommy Trinder, Fred Emney, Jack Buchanan, Richard Tauber and comedian Nat Jackley. His appearance as star of the hit show *Roll Out the Barrel* was the subject of a special report due to its interruption by an air raid during which the audience remained. One of the main gimmicks of the show was to treat the audience to a beer just before the final curtain after the second house! On that occasion when Birkenhead was taking a pounding until the early hours of the morning, war weary patrons joined the cast on the stage and an additional supply of beer had to be obtained.

Then came the glittering post war era with a host of American stars, Roy Rogers brought Trigger, then came Danny Kaye, Bob Hope, Bing Crosby and Ol' blue

eyes, Frank Sinatra. In the 1950s came Eric and Ernie (Morecambe and Wise), Ted Heath and his music band shows, Wee Georgie Wood and Jimmy Clitheroe. The Swinging Sixties was notable for a non-stop line up of top pop stars and entertainers including the Beatles, who appeared at the Empire several times. The *Royal Command Performance* before the Queen and Prince Charles featured a glittering array of Merseyside talent highlighted the seventies, but a riot marred an appearance of the Rolling Stones.

This was the beginning of a difficult period with closure rumours turning to black reality in July 1977 when Moss Empires reviewed plans to dispose of the theatre, which incredibly had made a loss over the previous five years. Fortunately Merseyside County Council stepped in and after careful consideration of the respective values of the Empire and the Royal Court, decided in favour of the former, due to its greater potential and adaptability. Moss Empires readily agreed to keep the theatre open while negotiations continued and in April 1979, the last of their provincial Empires was taken over by the Merseyside County Council to be run by a trust board.

At one stage it appeared that the rescue operation was doomed to flounder on the rocks of a government decision to axe the Arts Council's Housing the Arts fund by nearly half. The M.C.C. then championed a national campaign to save the large touring theatres, the government relented and the Arts Council received cash to save the Empire.

By October 1979, £330,000 had been spent back stage on improvements to what the council's director of touring, Mr. Jack Phipps described as potentially the most exciting theatre in the country, and in 1980 another £350,000 was spent in converting that potential into reality. When the Empire reopened, the first phase of the improvements included a quadraphonic sound system and lighting facilities equal to those at the New York Metropolitan, whilst new dressing rooms brought the artists' accommodation up to 140.

Later, phase II of the improvements was carried out during a hectic 17 weeks' closure, when the stage was extended, also

the orchestra pit to accommodate an 84 piece symphony orchestra. At the time, redecoration revealed long hidden joys of the original plasterwork designs, and the entire seating, then numbering 2,312 was re-upholstered.

Whilst the Empire has always been capable of attracting artists appropriate to its great size, due to the technical improvements of the early 1980s, the finest and most extravagant productions can be accommodated to the best advantage. During the first half of 1993, after many years under the ownership of Apollo Leisure U.K. Ltd., the Empire was stated to be on course for breaking all box office records for the second successive year, with a programming policy of such varied entertainments as sell-out star musicals, opera, ballet, plays, comedy and pop shows by first class companies.

1938 ROYAL COURT THEATRE, Roe Street

Construction of the new Royal Court Theatre commenced in March 1938, following the demolition of the old theatre of the same name. The architect was James B. Hutchins of Messrs. Wainwright and Co. of Lord Street whose plans provided for the building to occupy the site of 1,252 square yards. Adjacent to Roe Street, the main frontage, 142ft in length, curves at the right to the 82ft frontage to Great Charlotte Street. The height to the eaves is 82ft and the basement floor is 12ft below ground level.

The elevations are faced with a warm shade of red Blockley facing bricks, with pleasantly contrasting cream Ackwork stone dressings and Aberdeen granite architraves to the main entrance and exits. Above the principal entrance to the right of the Roe Street elevation, a striking architectural feature is formed with red bricks in vertical lines, relieved by stone dressings, with a similar feature on the Great Charlotte Street frontage, emphasises the considerable height of the building. Carved stone masks repre-

PROGRAMME

ROYAL COURT THEATRE
LIVERPOOL

Messrs HOWARD and WYNDHAM LTD.

Managing Director : Stewart Cruikshank

with booking offices was paved with San Stefano marble, and bordered with green and black Issoric marble. The walls were decorated with light toned figured walnut with panels and finished with a marble skirting. A most attractive feature was the fireplace for electric heating, with handsome surround in marble and engraved mirrors with bands of coloured glass. The appearance of this area, as other parts of the theatre, was enhanced by indirect lighting, shielded by cornices and pilasters. Therein a wall plaque summarised the history of entertainment on the site as follows - Cooke's New Circus 27th February 1826, remodelled - Cooke's Royal Amphitheatre of Arts, 1830, remodelled Royal Court Theatre reopened September 1881. Acquired by Robert Arthur Theatres Ltd. 1897. Theatre destroyed by fire 1933. Rebuilt and opened October 1938.

An additional advance booking hall with entrance in Great Charlotte Street was decorated in a similar style to that of the main foyer.

The auditorium was designed with two principal requirements, that the patrons would be able to see the performance without obstruction, and hear without straining. These were achieved to a high degree due to the arrangement of the seating, the absence of pillars, and the shallow curve of the circle, which enabled patrons at the side of the stalls to obtain as complete a view of the stage as those seated in the centre. The excellent acoustics were improved by the setting of the proscenium full width between the flanking splayed walls. The

senting Comedy and Tragedy adorn the area above the entrances on both elevations and for the comfort of queuing patrons, a canopy extends along the main portion of these. Although with the exception of the main entrance, the principal architectural features of the exterior remain, the following description of the interior is as reported at the time of opening.

Passing through one of the line of doors in the main entrance, flanked with Aberdeen granite facing, the entrance hall

ROYAL COURT THEATRE.
Box Office 10 to 8. Tel. Royal 5163/4.
TO-NIGHT, 7.30. MATS. WED. & SAT. 2.30.
LEE EPHRAIM presents the WORLD'S PREMIERE
CICELY & JACK
COURTNEIDGE HULBERT
IN
"UNDER YOUR HAT"
A New Musical Comedy.

MONDAY NEXT, Oct. 24th. FOR TWO WEEKS
Evenings 7.30. Matinees Wed. and Sat. at 2.30.
TOM ARNOLD, LTD., presents the
NOEL COWARD
SUCCESS.
"OPERETTE."
PEGGY IVY
WOOD. ST. HELIER.
PRICES (All Performances):—Stalls 7/6, 6/-; P
Stalls 3/6; Grand Circle 6/-, 4/6; Balcony 2/6
1/6. Matinees: Stalls 6/-, 4/6; Pt Stalls 2/6
Grand Circle 5/-, 3/-; Balcony 2/-, 1/-.

proscenium was most imposing with gilded carved plaster work around the edge, and adorned by attractively embroidered drapes and elegant pelmet, the whole being enhanced by the surrounding recess illuminated by concealed lighting. The finely decorated splayed walls featured at either side, a first floor box, surmounted by an arch, below a gilded decorative feature, above which the curved, coffered ceiling extended across. The boxes were fitted with pelmet and drapes appropriate to those of the proscenium, and the fronts with gilded, intricately carved designs in fibrous plaster, constituted an extension, via a curved bay, from the circle. Further concealed lighting extending across the curved ceiling bordered the ante-proscenium walls, whilst beyond a short splayed section which incorporated the front stalls and circle exits, decoration was by panelling above the dado, and above the upper circle, gilded rubs extended across the ceiling.

The total seating capacity of 1,612 was divided as follows - stalls 703, grand circle 403, upper circle 494 and 6 in each of the two boxes.

The stage, 62ft in width and 45ft deep, only 5ft less than the exceptional width of the old Royal Court's stage, provided every facility for the presentation of all types of theatrical productions. It was described as a glorious theatre from the producer's point of view for it was not too big, nor was it too small, and satisfied the demand of even the greediest of musical comedy or revue producers.

An elaborate counterweight system enabled 87 sets of scenery to be handled, and in accordance with modern ideas and requirements, a revolving stage was provided, and there were 19 dressing rooms for the accommodation of the artists.

A lounge furnished with table and chairs, where refreshments could be obtained, and a 50ft long standing bar were sited below the auditorium, and as in the upper entrances, decorative woodwork was effectively used, in this area with olive ash and figured walnut, whilst large mirrors were spaced around. Access to the upper parts of the theatre was by a metal balustraded, marble staircase, which curved

THE
ROYAL COURT THEATRE
—— LIVERPOOL ——
✦

Official Opening Ceremony
BY
Alderman M. CORY-DIXON, Lord Mayor of Liverpool
THURSDAY, OCTOBER 13th, 1938

ROYAL COURT THEATRE

around a central marble column.

The opening of the new Royal Court Theatre on 13th October 1938 was a notable event in the city with such strong theatrical traditions. There was an official reception attended by the Lord Mayor of Liverpool, Alderman M. Corey Dixon, who after a speech to the audience from the stage,

PROSCENIUM

BASEMENT
LOUNGE

formally declared the theatre open. The opening production was the new musical comedy Un*der Your Hat* with a cast headed by the famous team, Cicely Courtneidge and Jack Hulbert.

The theatre was the enterprise of the Robert Arthur Theatre Company, the proprietor's of the old Royal Court, then in association with the well known theatre proprietors, Messrs. Howard and Wyndham. the directorate included the famous producer, Mr. C. B. Cochran, who also addressed the audience stating that the opening could not have come at a better time due to the revival of drama throughout the country.

The Royal Court was successful for many years with the leading companies presenting opera, ballet, musical comedies, also comedy and dramatic plays featuring the famous stars of the time. In 1941, then under the sole control of Howard & Wyndham Ltd, the theatre missed destruction during the blitz, when a bomb exploded outside the stage door.

The late 1960s was noted as the beginning of a particularly difficult period in the history of theatre, which despite closures followed by reopenings with expectations of success, the theatre never really recovered for a sufficient length of time to indicate long term survival. The uncertain future was evident by the fact that in the year ended 28th February 1970, the loss of £853,000 represented an increase of £508,000 over that of the previous year.

Following closure in May 1970, the Royal Court reopened successfully on 20th October with Kenneth More and a strong cast in *The Winslow Boy*, but prior to this, after mounting a personal campaign to save the theatre, Liverpool comedian Ken Dodd, who had been voted Show Business Personality of the Variety Club of Great Britain, gave it the kiss of life by his arrangement with Bernard Delfont, managing director of E.M.I. to take over the theatre for four months from Christmas 1970 during the run of the *Ken Dodd Laughter Spectacular*. The success of this was guaranteed in advance, Ken Dodd being among the few comedians who had ever been able to create box office records by the sheer magnetism of his name.

The show provided a much needed boost for the theatre, apparently making possible, Howard and Wyndham's plans for 1971 to include the country's leading touring companies in two, four weeks' seasons at a cost of £60,000. But due to the insufficient number of stage attractions, Howard & Wyndham entered into a five years' contract with Mr. Alan Hutchinson of Hutchinson's Cinemas Ltd. for films to be shown for at least six months of the year including the summer season. It transpired however that 1971 was devoted to 'live' entertainment, the Liverpool corporation then having refused planning permission for the construction of a cinema projection room at the rear of the stalls. This was later permitted, resulting in a loss of 80 seats, and at that time a £10,000 facelift changed the colour scheme in the auditorium from predominantly brown to green and gold.

Howard & Wyndham's announced a sensational Family Film Season, which commenced on 29th May 1972 with good attendances for Walt Disney's *Fantasia* with admission at 30p, 50p and 60p to the performances at 2.00pm, 5.00pm and 8.00pm. The season which included reruns of notable films ended on 30th September, and 'live' entertainment returned on 2nd October with the comedy play *She Was Only An Admiral's Daughter* with Leslie Crowther and Dilys Watling heading the cast, which although attracting over 4,000 patrons in one week, the theatre remained in the red following losses on other shows.

Continuing with a varied selection of 'live' entertainment, supplemented by films, the Royal Court survived into 1976, when the theatre manager, David Liddy, announced the cancellation of all the summer and autumn shows, and formal notice of closure on 22nd May 1976 was given by the company to the staff's union N.A.T.K.E. Performances during the final week were by the English National Opera Company.

Considering it to be no longer a viable proposition, Howard and Wyndham's offered the theatre for sale at a figure of about £90,000 to the Merseyside County Council, who set up to take it over, the Royal Court Theatre and Arts Trust, with as Chairman, Sir Harry Livermore, and including

such diverse celebrities as Sir Harold Wilson and Ken Dodd. The Royal Court, if only temporarily, again came to life as hundreds of people clamoured to buy tickets for the Christmas 1978 Ken Dodd Laughter Show. Despite its great success, however, after the end of its run, followed by several plays, the theatre closed again on 23rd June 1979 due to financial difficulties.

Since it had been decided that the Empire should stage productions of opera, ballet and other shows by the leading companies, the Arts Council were uninterested and unwilling to participate in the future of the Royal Court as a theatre. The reopening on 2nd June 1980 for a season of music and drama was due only to the taking up of a lease by Max Fine of the Isle of Man based Douglas Entertainments Company. It compensated for the temporary closure of the Empire for improvements, but would not otherwise have taken place, for in the absence of public funds, continuance by the Trust was not possible.

After a short time, two former Liverpool taxi drivers, Alan Knipe and Joe Beckett had become sub-lessees of the trouble torn theatre, and in an attempt to improve its fortunes, instituted a complete change in the type of entertainment to rock and pop concerts. Nevertheless the year 1980 ended promisingly with a return to more conventional entertainment, and there were massive advance bookings to the amount of £20,000 for the Christmas version of *Ted Roger's Dusty Bin*, but this ended suddenly on 23rd December, due to outstanding debts of £50,000.

Despite financial and other difficulties, including a damaging flood in 1981, the theatre survived to become a leading rock music venue, playing host to internationally famous artists such as David Bowie, R.E.M., George Michael and local noteables including local pop group Frankie Goes To Hollywood.

The beginning of a new era for the theatre began in 1992, when due to the efforts of Merseyside historian Keith Newton the theatre was granted the status of a Grade II listed building by the Department of the Environment. In May 1995 it was announced that the Royal Court was to be redecorated, having been the chosen location of a derelict theatre in the plot of one of the television series Lovejoy, starring Ian MacShane.

Following this, drama returned during week commencing 25th March 1996, when the first play for nearly 25 years was Frank McGuiness's *Observe The Sons of Ulster* produced by Dublin's Abbey Theatre. For ten years under the direction of chief executive Simon Geddes, up to 70 rock concerts a year have been staged, but dependent upon fund raising to the extent of over £4m to provide improved facilities, the aim is also to present the varied range of entertainment for which the theatre was once famous.

1964
EVERYMAN THEATRE,
Hope Street

In about 1834 one Reverend R. Aitken, a Church of England minister, became a revivalist preacher and his followers erected a chapel in Hope Street. But his popularity waned and four years later the chapel became an orthodox church, St. John The Evangelist. When this church closed in 1853 it was converted for use as a public leisure and concert hall and became the venue of the principal Mersey concerts. This became in 1912 the Hope Hall Cinema, which survived under the control of several proprietors and lessees until 1959 and following a period of closure the use as a cinema was continued in 1961 by Mr. Leslie Blond, proprietor of the Continental Cinema, Wallasey, who was Chairman of the Liverpool North West and North Wales Association of Independent cinemas.

A £35,000 scheme of alterations and improvements then included the removal of the seating, except for a few church pews in the balcony, and the construction of an apron stage and dressing room to provide for the possible long term project of an experimental theatre. With seating for 750, it was to be run on theatre lines, with

bookable seats for the foreign films and a coffee interval. It opened with its former name, the Hope Hall on 8th May 1961 with Ingmar Bergman's *So Close To Life* supported by *The Little Island* at separate performances 6.15pm and 8.30pm to which the prices of admission were 3/-, 4/-, 4/6d, and pews at 1/6d. On 10th December 1961 the change of name was made to the Everyman Cinema, but probably sooner than had been anticipated, came the change to a theatre, the cinema closing on 15th November 1963 with the film *Sons and Lovers* starring Trevor Howard.

The building was closed until August 1964, when the work of full conversion to a theatre was commenced. The new semi-circular stage with seating on three sides extended 15 feet into the 650 seat auditorium, with the object of making the audience feel more closely indentified with the productions, which were to be fully costumed, but with the minimum of scenery.

The original company was born of an idea that there was a gap in the theatre pattern, the founders were three young students, who arrived in Liverpool from different parts of the country. One, Martin Jenkins was nominated as Britain's top student actor at the 1962 drama festival, and after completing 18 months with the Royal Shakespeare company at Stratford-on-Avon, conveyed his theatre founding enthusiasm to Peter James and Terry Hands when they were still students at Birmingham University. They were joined by Michael Freeman, who after leaving the University, became general manager, whilst Martin Jenkins became the artistic director. Their aim was to offer adult playgoers the chance to see dramas from the Greek classics to Pinter, performed by a young but experienced company, three evenings weekly, but also to create a new audience of schoolchildren at five matinees weekly of plays chosen to fit in with school requirements. Initially it was this aspect which won them a hearing and support from the local authorities, for in addition to a grant, Liverpool gave to the Everyman, a payment of £3,000.

In addition the education committee guaranteed £400 to be given in the form of

an allowance of 1/6d to interested pupils attending the matinees for the admission price of 2/6d.

During the summer of 1964, the Everyman Theatre company called for volunteers to assist in the work of adapting the former cinema to its new purpose. The call was answered by a score or more of students and schoolgirls who gave up a fortnight of their school holidays for the work of cleaning, painting, sawing, also sewing for those assigned to the dress designer.

The board set up to run the Everyman, had as Chairman, Alderman Harry Livermore, who then also held a similar position in the Royal Philharmonic Society and the directorate included the owner of the building, Leslie Blond.

Described as the bravest theatrical venture in Liverpool for some time, and an addition to the cultural life of the city, the Everyman Theatre opened on 28th September 1964, with a matinee for which the appropriate choice of play was Shakespeare's *Henry IV* this being the company's contribution to the quarter centenary year, and the school's G.C.E. and 'O' level play. But in order to avoid the tag of "The Children's Theatre", the play in the evening was chosen for a wider audience. *The Caretaker* by Harold Pinter, was attended by the Lord Mayor of Liverpool, Alderman Louis Caplan and other distinguished guests, and open to the public at a guinea a seat.

With plays to follow such as Ibsen's *An Enemy of the People* it was stated that in the evening, the Everyman would be catering for the same type of people who attend the Playhouse, but with the exception of the opening night, evening bookings were well below expectations. After only 9 months there was a crisis appeal for £1,000 to keep the company in existence with the alternative of immediate closure. The appeal was fortunately successful, and the theatre thereafter survived through good and bad times with financial troubles persisting until 1970, when the Arts Council stepped in with a grant to supplement that of the corporation.

During the early seventies, the reputation of the theatre was enhanced by a

popular choice of plays, reaching a peak of success in 1975/76, described as a miracle year by the then Chairman, Alan Durband. This did not however diminish the call, which had originated in 1970 for a new theatre in the city at a cost of half a million pounds. Supported by Chairman Harry Livermore, there was an opinion that if the Everyman could not be re-housed it would not survive. No decision was made by the Liverpool Corporation regarding the new plans, and in Autumn 1976 a public appeal for £280,000 was launched for a comprehensive facelift of the theatre. Eventually a total of £307,000 was raised, and the Everyman was closed in January 1977. A former factory in Fleet Street became the temporary home of the company, from which they continued by taking the theatre to the people

via working men's clubs and various halls during the construction of the present Everyman Theatre in Hope Street.

1975
THE CIVIC HALL,
Crosby Road, North,
Waterloo

Coinciding with the year when the Metropolitan Borough of Sefton was granted its Royal Charter, the new Civic Hall took its place together with the Arts Centre, Southport and the Concert Hall in the Bootle Town Hall as a fitting venue for drama, music, dance also civic and private require-

ments. The need for such a hall in the district had been apparent for many years during which operatic and drama productions had been staged in the Town Hall, Waterloo and the Alexandra Hall, Crosby, but those of the Waterloo & District Amateur Operatic Society, were for many years seen on the stage of the Winter Gardens cinema in Church Road. Although designed for multi-purpose use, neither of the former public halls possessed appropriate stage facilities, and when the Central Library was completed in 1968, it was originally planned to incorporate a public hall as part of a cultural complex. Due to financial restrictions it was then decided to erect a library only, but with plans appropriate to the addition of a hall at a later date.

The lack of theatrical facilities became very apparent when the newly formed Crosby Arts Association brought artists of international repute to the area, and in November 1972 the scheme proceeded for the erection of a public hall in the position originally proposed. Accordingly plans were prepared by the Chief Architect, Mr. G. Ronald Mason, B. Arch (Hons) A.R.I.B.A., to meet the requirements that the new hall must be multi-purpose for the envisaged activities of opera and drama, ballets, concerts and recitals, lectures, exhibitions and meetings, dances and film performances of an educational nature.

Although the size of the hall was limited by cost, site restrictions and the desire to achieve an intimate character, it was nevertheless considered that a seating capacity of 400 would be adequate for most functions. The multi-purpose necessitated that the seating should be movable, the chairs selected being of the upholstered stacking type. When cleared away this left the lower area with sprung maple floor to accommodate 250 dancers, whilst the rear part, raised 2ft. 6in, could be used either with normal seating for stage performance, or with tables and chairs as a sitting out area for the dancers. The wide fan-shaped plan of the auditorium was considered to be most practical due to the limited depth of the site, and brought the audience as near to the stage as possible. On the side walls a series of alcoves with fixed seating for use by spectators at dances, was formed by projecting fin walls. In addition to being a design feature, the fins also served to conceal the air intake grilles, and movable spot lights were mounted at various points above the ceiling of the alcoves.

The stage was described as commodious and well equipped with safety curtain, scenery fly tower and access bay, and at the front a movable apron stage was provided, which could be fitted over the orchestra pit, designed to accommodate approximately 28 instrumentalists when the latter is not in use. To assist with the forward reflection of the sound, a full width sounding board, suspended over the apron and angled down, forms the upper edge of the proscenium. Above the rear of the auditorium a spotlight room was constructed, which also serves for the projection of films by 16mm projectors on to a screen at the rear of the stage.

Adjacent to the rear of the auditorium is the main foyer with licensed bar, booking office, cloakroom and a stairway to the first floor refreshment room also on this floor is the lecture hall with accommodation for 100 people, in which is a small platform and screen for the showing of slides and films from the projection room at the rear of the hall.

With reference to the exterior, every effort was made to ensure that the theatre harmonised with the existing library, the circular library tower and cupola standing on the main axis of the new hall, fulfilling its original purpose in dominating and uniting the two buildings. The Civic Hall was built by contractors, R. Costain & Sons (Liverpool) Ltd., at a cost of £300,000 by the Crosby Corporation without Arts Council or other outside support.

The official opening by the Mayor of Sefton, Councillor E. Rowland Bell took place on 6th October 1975 when a Gala celebrity recital was given by the internationally renowned soprano, Victoria de los Angeles, and the concert also inaugurated the Crosby Arts Festival 1975. The Civic was soon being called the other Albert Hall, the manager being Mr. Albert Howell, whose arts involvement on Merseyside had spanned more than 30 years, during which, due to his proven ability at engaging big name artists, and organising arts festivals, he had been named in that year, Concerts Organiser for Sefton. Under his able management until retirement in recent years, the Civic Hall presented the great variety of entertainment and activities for which it was intended and in recent years has been continued by his successors.

1977
THE NEW EVERYMAN THEATRE,
Hope Street

This could justifiably be described as a new building, although in fact, behind the completely new facade the outer walls and the roof of the old theatre remained. This extensive scheme was at a cost of £330,000 of which £125,000 was contributed by the Arts Council, £30,000 by the English Tourist Board and the remainder by appeals on Merseyside.

Architect, Joseph Parker of the Anthony Clark partnership stated that although the original building was in good structural condition with magnificent timber trusses spanning 60 to 70ft, a series of alterations since the conversion to the Hope Hall cinema in 1912, had each left it in slightly worse condition. In this respect however, the altered frontage had deteriorated to the greatest extend and was demolished.

Clashing with Hope Street's more sober Georgian Classical architecture, the new frontage was of plain surfaces without ornamentation, and relieved only by a full width ripple effect, red neon Everyman electric sign, this upper part of the frontage projecting over the line of entrances to form a narrow canopy.

The new planning of the interior dispensed with many undesirable features, such as the area nearly resembling a coal hole, which was used for a dressing room! The eight foot by four foot so called Black Hole of Calcutta in which the administrative staff laboured, which although formerly contributing to the raffish and slightly seedy charm of the place, were a definite disadvantage for people working there. The new stage was constructed on the level of the former circle, making permanent the temporary structure erected shortly before the theatre closed in 1976. At the front the space between the stage and seating, which the company named The Great Hole could be left, covered over to extend the stage area, or used to provide seating additional to the 400 capacity, arranged on three sides of the stage. Below the auditorium the former stalls area provided space for dressing rooms with the vital addition of showers for the artists, whilst for the audience, the re-styled Everyman was a more comfortable experience with the restaurant extended to seat 150, and downstairs drinks and snacks were available at the brasserie bar.

Almost thirteen years to the day after

its original opening, the new Everyman theatre opened with a flourish and a fanfare on 21st September 1977, when the capacity audience included among the distinguished guests, Lord Selwyn Lloyd, Sir Charles Groves and singer Barbara Dickson. The opening attraction was Chris. Bond's Liverpool adaption of John Gay's *The Beggar's Opera,* which brought forth the press comment that whilst beggars may say that money is rotten, it has turned a shack into a theatre!

With regard to future productions, chairman Alan Durband took the opportunity to stress that the company would be specifically aiming for a more up-market audience, those lined up for the new season including *Yeatsev and the Whale* (a study of the whaling industry in Bromborough until the war), Bill Morrison's *Flying Blind* (about Ulster), and the pantomime *Cinderella* at Christmas.

The appeal of the Everyman was principally to the young including students and intended to provide an alternative to the normal stock repertoire of time honoured plays at the Playhouse and Royal Court theatres. For some time the Everyman gained support with this policy, but during the 1980s, the Playhouse Studio theatre began to erode its traditional audience, and for the first time it became questionable whether Liverpool really needed two home-producing repertory companies. In the early 1990s with further decreasing audiences, financial difficulties arose, and in the spring of 1993, due to dwindling income, the five

Merseyside local authorities were unable to match Arts Council funds, which during the last year of operation had amounted to £450,000 to the Everyman. Not wishing to continue under these circumstances, the Arts Council chose to support the Playhouse which had the advantage of private backing by West End based Merseyside producer, Bill Kenwright.

The Everyman was saved for the short time by a £100,000 gesture of goodwill, provided by the Playhouse, but in October, with debts stated as £70,000, survival depended upon the immediate release of £80,000 funds by the Arts Council. This was however on condition that the Everyman board of directors agreed to a new artistic policy which would include outside companies to stage performances. This was refused by the board, who were unwilling to surrender artistic control, and in mid October, the high price was the closure of the theatre and liquidation of assets.

The Everyman, which has been described as being one of Britain's most distinguished theatres, might have been permanently lost to Liverpool's playgoers, but for the proprietors, during the previous 20 years, of the basement bistro, Paddy Byrne, and business partner, Dave Scott, who acquired the freehold of the auditorium and annexe for the sum of £260,000. The stage was leased to a new board and the curtain again rose on 15 February 1994 with the Liverpool based Kaboodle Theatre company's award winning production of Shakespeare's *King Lear*. The first attraction of a six week season of visiting plays and concerts.

With anticipated support of the Arts Council and Merseyside local authorities, Kaboodle is one of many local companies who are to contribute to the Everyman's programming. In accordance with the latest trend to fund individual groups, the new board stated their preference for this programme policy rather than the theatre should be a venue for visiting shows from London and elsewhere. With this policy, favoured especially by young supporters of the theatre, the Everyman continues.

1980 UNITY THEATRE, Hope Place

Merseyside Unity Theatre originally referred to the company rather than as in recent years, a specific location, and in its heyday before World War II, made great contributions in support of Spanish democracy and socialism in the struggle against fascism. This theatre of the left, as it was termed, presented plays at various situations including the David Lewis theatre, the County Hall, Bootle and Blair Hall in Walton. In the immediate post war years, the first permanent venue was at 62 Mount Pleasant, Liverpool, where former Labour MP, the late Eric Heffer was the Chairman, and also carried out the duties of stage carpenter. The theatre was stated to have a pocket handkerchief size stage in the very small auditorium, but the plays were considered to be excellent, and the standard of performances constantly high. Flourishing among the working people in the area, it made a great contribution to the work of the Labour movement on Merseyside.

The present Unity Theatre, located at 1 Hope Place occupies the ground floor of the building which was originally a mid-Victorian synagogue. This was converted in 1980 into a small theatre with the status of a studio venue to accommodate an audience of 140 on a raked floor around the approximately 33ft by 24 ft. performing area. This is illuminated by spotlights fitted to the straight ceiling, and dressing rooms are provided at the side of the area, with music to accompany the performances by reel to reel and cassette tape systems. During 1989/90 renovations and improvement to the foyer have been carried out, and catering facilities consist of a coffee bar, and a licensed bar, which is open in the evenings only for the performance, normally at 8.00pm.

The theatre is funded by the Arts Council and various local authorities, offering a mixed programme policy of professional/aspiring professional and local groups presenting programmes covering drama, dance, mime, new writing and ethnic arts. Often written by new unknown local writers and performed by a combination of out of work actors and hopefuls amateurs, productions have been described as of varying standards. It is noteworthy however, that the original stage version of *A Letter To Brezhnev* was first seen at the Unity Theatre before it becam a much acclaimed film.

The Unity Theatre survives at this time, in the mid 1990s, and being the last to be opened in the Liverpool area, brings to an end this history of *The Liverpool Stage*.

INDEX